A 4 R

Øsen 584

90p.

Carl Becker: On History & the Climate of Opinion

BY CHARLOTTE WATKINS SMITH

Southern Illinois University Press
CARBONDALE AND EDWARDSVILLE

Feffer & Simons, Inc.
LONDON AND AMSTERDAM

Library of Congress Cataloging in Publication Data

Smith, Charlotte Watkins.
        Carl Becker: on history & the climate of opinion.
        (Arcturus books, AB112)
        "Originally written as a doctoral dissertation for
. . . the University of Chicago."
        Bibliography: p.
        1.   Becker, Carl Lotus, 1873–1945.
[D15.B33S52   1973]   973.3′07′2024 [B]   72–11826
ISBN 0–8093–0632–8

**ARCT
URUS
BOOKS** ®

Copyright © 1956 by Cornell University
All rights reserved
Reprinted by arrangement with Cornell University Press
Arcturus Books Edition April 1973
This edition printed by offset lithography
in the United States of America

Preface

THIS study was begun as a work in American historiography, not as an attempt at biography. I intended to deal with historical relativism as developed and expressed by Carl Becker. I did not intend to concern myself very much with his life, which appeared to have been quite uneventful, or with his political writings or opinions except insofar as they influenced his beliefs and his practice in writing history. All of these intentions, and the assumption on which they were based, turned out to be naïve. The material as it grew failed to fit into the pigeonholes I had provided—pigeonholes labeled with appropriate rubrics: the man, the teacher, the writer, the historian, the citizen, the philosopher, and so on. First, I could not disentangle the writer from the historian; next, Becker's beliefs about democracy came to seem entirely germane to his beliefs about how history should be written; finally, Becker's life ceased to appear uneventful except in the most external sense. In the realm of imagination Becker's life was exciting—a tale of difficulties overcome, of tragedy and pain accepted, the high adventure of a courageous and discriminating mind confronting the universe without fear and without illusion. What Becker was, what he did, and what he thought about all manner of things were somehow all of a piece. But it was not at all a simple piece. Simplicity there was in him, but it was the achieved simplicity that lies beyond complexity.

All of this has, of course, been shown in longer or shorter compass by his friends and former students. Guy Stanton Ford, George Sabine, Leo Gershoy, and Louis Gottschalk have written appreciative articles, and Carl Horwich and David Hawke have done master's theses on Becker. All except the last of these, however, wrote before Becker's papers were available. In 1950 David Hawke of the University of Wisconsin very effectively used the file of correspondence and manuscripts at Cornell. Since that time, fortunately, a good many more of Becker's letters have been added to the collection, and all of his research notes have been made available. I have made extensive use of Mr. Hawke's thesis, particularly his chapter on Becker's years as a student at the University of Wisconsin and his bibliography of Becker's writings. He has also very generously let me see many letters which he received from Becker's students in answer to his queries. The papers now in the Cornell University Library have not been thoroughly explored before, and they offer the possibility of a fuller understanding of Becker's methods of work and ways of thinking.

Becker has a fourfold place in American thought. First, his commanding position among twentieth-century American historians is unquestioned. Whether the object is to praise the relativistic trend of American historiography (as it was with Harry Elmer Barnes in his *History of Historical Writing*) or to deprecate it (as it was with Maurice Mandelbaum in his *Problem of Historical Knowledge*), Becker's name is prominent in any study of the subject.

Second, Becker is one of the very few historians of our day accounted a writer, a man of letters, someone worth reading for pleasure. He is as much worth studying (and, in fact, appears in college readers about as often) as some of the nineteenth-century essayists who are read for their "style."

Third, Becker is, I believe, unique among American historians in being often claimed by professional philosophers as one of themselves. They made the claim with some diffidence—not wishing to ruin his reputation—but they made it unequivocally all the same. "A critical historian who is also, though he would perhaps not admit it, a philosopher," so runs the description of Becker by Arthur E. Murphy.[1]

Fourth, although Becker was a man of thought, he had sufficient imagination and judgment to appreciate the life of action and to allow for the compromises forced upon those who are making history instead of studying it. Becker understood American politics as few can who have not taken active part in it, and he perhaps helped to clarify the political ideas of a number of public men who were enthusiastic readers of his books. He certainly helped to shape the political beliefs of great numbers of American citizens who learned most of what they know of modern history from his high-school textbook.

Rolling all four reasons into one, one finds in Becker Emerson's idea of a scholar—man thinking; one finds in his work an illustration of Bacon's faith—"The images of men's wits and knowledges remain . . . exempted from the wrong of time. Neither are they fitly to be called images, because they generate still, and cast their seeds in the minds of others." [2]

This study was originally written as a doctoral dis-

[1] *The Uses of Reason* (New York: Macmillan, 1943), p. 207.

[2] Francis Bacon, *Advancement of Learning*, ed. William Aldis Wright (4th ed.; Oxford: Clarendon Press, 1891), p. 72.

Preface

sertation for the Department of History of the University of Chicago. I have had helpful criticism and suggestions from several friends and advisers. I am especially grateful to the members of my advisory committee—William T. Hutchinson, Louis Gottschalk, and Charner M. Perry —and to three others who have read most of the manuscript—the historian and former student of Carl Becker, Geoffrey Bruun; my husband, Gayle Smith; and my father-in-law, T. V. Smith.

Members of the Cornell University community have been unfailingly kind about answering questions, and the Cornell University Library has extended to me every convenience in using the Becker Papers and has generously given me permission to quote freely from them. I wish particularly to thank Mr. G. F. Shepherd, Jr., who has worked to extend the collection in time to benefit me, and Miss Gussie Gaskill, librarian of the Andrew D. White Collection, who knew Becker for many years as a student and friend.

For permission to quote from personal letters and from copyrighted publications I am grateful to the following: Justice Felix Frankfurter for letters written to Becker in 1935; Martha Dodd Stern for letters written by William E. Dodd to Becker; Mark Van Doren for letters written by Carl Van Doren to Becker; Val Lorwin for a letter written to David Hawke; *The Atlantic Monthly* for passages from "Detachment and the Writing of History"; *The American Historical Review* for quotations from "Mr. Wells and the New History" and from "Everyman His Own Historian"; *The Philosophical Review* for quotations from Becker's review of *The Problem of Historical Knowledge* by Maurice Mandelbaum; Alfred A.

Preface

Knopf for quotations from *Progress and Power* and from *The Declaration of Independence;* The Yale University Press for passages from *The Eve of the Revolution;* and *The William and Mary Quarterly* for permission to reprint Chapter IV.

C. W. S.

College Park, Maryland
August, 1955

Contents

Carl Becker: On History and the Climate of Opinion

I

Carl Becker's Life

*After I know not how long it dawned on me, and with what
a joyous sense of emancipation, that Turner wasn't, that no
university professor need be, merely a teacher. . . .*

*In this happy way I got a new idea of history. It was after
all no convention agreed upon to be learned by rote, but just
the infinitely varied action and thought of men who in past
times had lived and struggled and died for mean or great
objects. It was in short an aspect of life itself, and as such
something to be probed into, thought about, written about.*[1]

CARL BECKER's forebears were in many ways typical
early Americans. His father's Dutch and German ances-
tors had settled in New York State, "probably in the
eighteenth century." His mother's people—English and
Irish—also had settled in New York; he had "no idea
when." Like most pioneers, they turned their thoughts

[1] Carl Becker, "Frederick Jackson Turner," *Everyman His Own
Historian: Essays on History and Politics* (New York: Appleton-
Century-Crofts, 1935), pp. 196–199. This essay was reprinted from
Howard W. Odum (ed.), *Masters of the Social Sciences* (New
York: Henry Holt, 1927).

1

Carl Becker

to the future, toward building a new life in a new country, and memories of family history and bygone cultures faded rapidly; Becker's paternal great-grandfather could not speak anything but German; his father, Charles, could not speak anything but English.[2]

Charles Dewitt Becker served for three years in the Union Army; then, like many another Civil War veteran, he decided to go west where he could find cheaper land. In 1867, in Carthage, New York, he married Almeda Sarvay and took her first to Illinois, and then on to Black Hawk County, Iowa, "where he bought eighty acres of as good farm land as there is anywhere to be found."[3] In a few months his brother-in-law, Lotus Sarvay, hearing good reports from Iowa, came out from New York and bought an adjoining farm.

The Beckers prospered and were able to triple the size of their farm within a few years. They throve in a thriving country. They were prominent citizens in the community and leading members of the Methodist church. In politics, Charles Becker, believing, naturally enough, in voting as he had shot, was always a staunch Republican.[4] Here on the Iowa farm Carl Lotus Becker,

[2] Becker, *The United States: An Experiment in Democracy* (New York: Harpers, 1920), p. 240.

[3] *Ibid.*

[4] Jessie Becker to Carl Becker [1940]. Becker's notes, manuscripts, and correspondence, left to the Cornell University Library at his death, have been arranged and classified by his old friend, Mr. E. R. B. Willis, and were first made available in 1949. The letter file contains incoming letters running back as far as 1896, but Becker rarely kept copies of his own letters, which he usually wrote in longhand. Through the co-operation of his correspondents many of his letters, either originals or photostatic copies, have

their only son, the second of four children, was born on September 7, 1873, and in this substantial, respected farm family he was raised.

He had some firsthand experience of frontier life. Although Iowans in the 1870's did not have Indian raids to worry about, they had troubles with the tribes that were left. If the Beckers left their farm for several hours, they were quite likely when they returned to find a party of wandering Indians in possession of the place. There they stayed, silent, staring, curious, and immovable until they had a mind to go. Carl acquired the pioneer's dislike of Indians very early and never entirely got over it. But he loved farm life and always looked back on his boyhood with nostalgia. He was a local champion at ice skating and remembered marvelous times out of doors in the Iowa winters; he remembered too, even more poignantly perhaps, the stacks of pancakes and syrup he used to eat.

When Carl was about eleven years old, his father let the farm to a tenant and moved his family into the nearby town of Waterloo. Here Carl attended grammar school and high school. Here also he discovered the public library and set out to consume it, assisted by an unusually perceptive librarian. Becker recalled later how she had behaved when he chose *Anna Karenina* from the shelf and asked her, "Is this a good book?"

The lady glanced at the title, then looked at me, over her spectacles, searchingly, sizing me up, no doubt wondering whether, for a boy of perhaps thirteen, *Anna Karenina* was

---

been added to the collection. All the letters hereafter referred to are in the Becker Papers unless otherwise indicated.

after all quite the thing. At last she said: "It's a very powerful book." Nothing else—a wise lady I've always thought.[5]

Although his family moved to town while he was still a youngster, Carl saw and did a good deal of real farming. He spent several summers with his Sarvay cousins, who continued to live on the farm adjoining the Becker place. "During the summers of 1888–91 I enjoyed the great pleasure of following a McCormic [*sic*] self-binder about a forty-acre oat field for ten hours a day, in the humble capacity of a 'shocker,'" he wrote in 1909. The new reaper impressed him greatly. Only a few years earlier he had seen his father "cut his wheat with the old fashioned reaper which raked a single unbound 'bundle' on the ground." [6] But something more than the novelty of new machinery attracted him; after one of these summers—following his sophomore year in high school—he wrote home in September that he had decided to quit school and work on the farm. His father, a man of intelligence and force of character, soon got him over that notion. Carl, according to his sister, was speedily "brought home and told with great emphasis that he must finish high school." [7]

Being a boy of "an exceptionally good disposition," Carl obediently returned to school. He found a new principal in charge that term, Miss Annie S. Newman, and from then on, his sister recalls, "all trouble was over." The troubles of his sophomore year had indeed been sur-

[5] Becker, "The Art of Writing," MS of an unpublished article in the Becker Papers.

[6] Becker to R. G. Thwaites, April 25, 1909 (Wisconsin State Historical Society).

[7] Miss Jessie Becker to author, March 14, 1952.

prising in a quiet, conscientious boy such as Carl nor-
mally was. He had even been temporarily expelled from
school in what his sister remembers as "his one and only
scrape." It hardly seems an expellable offense, even for
Iowa in the 1880's. He and his cousin, Leonard Sarvay,
returned a little late to school one day after morning
recess with playing cards pinned on their backs. For this
display of wickedness, apparently, they were expelled.
But the action did not stick. Carl's father "sent the boys
back with a note which caused the superintendent to tell
the boys to take their seats and forget the matter." [8] The
next year, under the new principal, Carl rapidly recovered his former interest in his studies and went on to
graduate from high school amid general expectations
that he would distinguish himself. In the fall of 1892 he
and his cousin entered Cornell College in Mount Vernon,
Iowa. The following year he transferred to the University
of Wisconsin.

His remark in his essay on Frederick Jackson Turner
that he "went to the University of Wisconsin for the same
reason that many boys go to one college or another—
because a high school friend of mine, whose cousin or
something had been 'at Madison,' was going there" had
perhaps better not be taken too literally. It was for reasons like those that he went to Cornell College. But his
sister tells us: "He hadn't been there very long before he
realized that he couldn't get what he wanted in a small
college, and his great desire was to go to Madison." [9]
The death of his cousin, his most intimate friend and
Cornell classmate, added to his desire to change schools.

Probably no more stimulating atmosphere could have

[8] *Ibid.*   [9] *Ibid.*

Carl Becker

been found at any American university in the 1890's than that at the growing University of Wisconsin. Very few schools had more distinguished faculties: Richard T. Ely, John Charles Freeman, Charles Homer Haskins, Frederick Jackson Turner—Becker studied with them all. New and controversial courses like sociology, psychology, and American literature were offered at Wisconsin, and Becker missed none of them.[10] Famous lecturers came to the campus, and Becker listened to them with critical attention. Touring repertory companies played frequently at the Madison opera house, and Becker sat in the gallery drinking in all the sights.

Becker took his first course with Turner in 1894. "Until then, I had never been interested in history; since then, I have never ceased to be so," Becker wrote to Turner in 1910.[11] This new and absorbing interest did not change the young Iowan's course of study noticeably. He had gone to the university hoping to become a writer; during his second year he determined to write history. He had started to take a broad course of study in literature, languages, and the social sciences, with a sprinkling of philosophy and mathematics, and he steadily continued taking it.

Becker was not one of the late-flowering geniuses whose teachers foolishly take them for dunderheads; nor was he one of the brilliant young men whose talents dazzle everyone from the beginning. He was too quiet and self-contained for that. He must have seemed to

[10] David Hawke, "Carl Becker," master's thesis, University of Wisconsin.

[11] Becker to Turner, May 15, 1910 (first draft). Presumably the letter actually sent is among the Turner Papers in the Huntington Library.

most of his classmates a prosaically good student. His scholastic record was uniformly good, showing a steady improvement from the solid B average of his freshman year to the straight A of his senior year, which he completed in 1896. It is a record so unswerving in direction, so invariable, so impeccable—his lowest grade was a 75 in English—that it might well represent the work of a stolid, unimaginative boy impelled by ambition or conscience to grind away at his books without letup and without digression, his eyes fixed upon a goal entirely clear. Such an estimation would be wide of the mark. Although Becker was a quiet, introverted youth and stolid in appearance, the appearance was deceptive. Whether anyone at the university suspected it or not, he suffered from the emotional strains that often throw college students into temporary despair and play havoc with their studies. That he suffered no such effects was surely owing to the methodical habits, self-discipline, and strong common sense that characterized him all his life —qualities that counterbalanced (and even counteracted) a mind too searching, an imagination too vivid, for comfort.

The only evidence in Becker's hand about his undergraduate years is in two notebooks in which he kept a combination journal and commonplace book from January, 1894, to May, 1895. Each bears the title "Wild Thoughts Notebook." They are not diaries; they do not pretend to chronicle his activities, but they do reflect his state of mind. These notebooks indicate that for the first two years he was at Wisconsin his aim was far from clear. He hankered to be a writer, but that was an uncertain business so far as making a living was concerned. He had his family to think about too—hard-working,

God-fearing people they were, convinced "of the advantage of possessing 'a good education'" and naturally expecting him to settle on a profession. But college for him seemed to open the whole "wide world of the human spirit," and he was reluctant to choose a tiny corner of it for his own and give up the rest. He had entered at Madison upon the "Civic-Historical" curriculum designed particularly for pre-law students, and he had shown at once that he could handle the work very well indeed. Nothing seemed to be in his way. He could make himself anything he liked—a lawyer, possibly in later life a judge. Small wonder that his father was puzzled and troubled to see him hesitating about a career without clear-cut plans. One of the "Wild Thoughts Notebooks" contains a dialogue between a father and son under the date line, "Waterloo, Ia., April 8, 1895":

Father (after long silence): Have they got a law school up there at Madison?

Son (wearily): Yes.

Father: How long does it take to get through?

Son: Why it's two years now I guess.

Father: (after short silence): Well, have you decided yet on what you'll do when you finish up there?

Son: No.

Father: (after long interval): Well, I suppose it's a question that takes some time and ain't very easy to decide, but I should almost think you'd want to decide pretty soon. You could work along in that direction then I should think.[12]

We can but think this conversation occurred between Carl Becker and his father, who did hope that Carl

[12] "Wild Thoughts Notebook," April 8, 1895, Becker Papers.

would be a lawyer.[13] Charles Becker is revealed here as a reserved man, unaccustomed to receiving or demanding confidences, anxious to be just in a matter he knows he little understands, but withal doggedly aware that life is not all study. The son, "weary" and rather stubbornly declining to volunteer a single remark to ease his father's misgivings, nevertheless records the scene faithfully and with a sympathetic touch. He seems to see the episode not as an example of officious interference by an insensitive parent but rather as an example of the loneliness of man's lot, where even father and son cannot communicate. Carl had always been an affable child "willing to do what his parents thought was for his best." [14] Here, perhaps for the first time, he had to disappoint his father seriously. Fortunately both his parents lived to see him win a high reputation as a historian. His mother died in 1915; his father in 1919.

Becker did not decide to major in history until some time after he had taken Turner's course. In the meantime he envied as well as despised the sublime confidence of certain bustling students whom he described as follows:

These are the fellows who have definite aims. They are certain just what they are going to do and how it is to be done. Moreover, they delight in telling you all about it. He studies so long, at this particular time he reads, so many hours in the gym. This much sleep, etc. etc. He tells you when this study will come in; how that one will follow; what he will do when he graduates, where he will go; what position he is after and

[13] Miss Jessie Becker to author, March 14, 1952.
[14] *Ibid.*

perhaps where he will board in five years. Everything is planned so; So it will be.[15]

This kind of student—the hustler—was at the opposite pole from Becker. He described delightfully and almost literally, one feels, for all his air of whimsey, the way he decided to become a professor:

The four years in college was to me a wonderful adventure in the wide world of the human spirit. . . . Suffice it to say that the four years were up before I had more than begun to get the lay of the land. Less than ever did I desire to return to the known world and tread in monotonous routine the dusty streets of Now and Here. How fine, I thought, to remain always in this unknown country! How fine not to have "to do" anything! And one day it dawned upon me that this was precisely the case of my admired professors. Here they were, confined for life in this delightful country of the mind, with nothing "to do," privileged to go on as best they could with the great adventure. From that moment I was a lost man. I was bound to become a professor.[16]

This must have been sometime in 1895. There is no record in the "Wild Thoughts Notebooks" of any decision about a career, but the last dated entry is in May, 1895. Already the detached, speculative quality of his mind was evident. The quieter he was, the more he heard; the more he heard, the more he learned about the fascinating human animal, and the fatter his notebooks grew. The notebooks reveal a very unadolescent sense of proportion in his view of his own and other people's problems.

[15] "Wild Thoughts Notebook," Oct. 18, 1894.
[16] Becker, "On Being a Professor," *Unpopular Review,* VII (April–June, 1917), 343.

He was highly aware of the flow of life around him. On all sides he saw men attempting to come to terms with the universe—not very successfully. For a while he kept going to the Methodist church out of habit, but he began to find its answers to the riddle of life less and less satisfactory and its members less and less congenial. By the spring of 1894 he had abandoned fundamentalist Christianity, in his mind at least, and had come to a semideistic position. He mused in his journal, March 5, 1894:

A man's religion is that secret part of his soul which is known to himself and God only. Christianity is an attempt to formulate religion.

Every man has a religion. It may be good or it may perhaps be bad, but it is no man's business but his own.

A man's religion is the best there is of him. The province of the Church is educational and charitable; but not reformatory. . . .

Don't try to reform men, it can't be done. Reform yourself. If every man and every woman who calls himself or herself a Christian would concentrate his whole energy upon the one point of reforming himself as far as it can be done, the world would be "saved" in less time than it takes an ordinary revivalist to work his congregation up to white heat.

Leo Tolstoi's definition of religion is that it is "man's relation to the universe." I think that is about equivalent to saying that it is his relation to his God.[17]

By August he had come to the conclusion that "people should teach children how to act and let them believe as they please." [18] "Less religion and more manners would increase the value of many 'very good' people," he

[17] "Wild Thoughts Notebook," March 5, 1894.
[18] *Ibid.,* Aug. 14, 1894.

added. Youthful snobbery, betrayed in a growing opinion that people of the greatest cultivation and sophistication were seldom Methodists, seems to have speeded up his estrangement from the religion of his childhood. When he attended a recital given in a Methodist church, he looked sharply at the audience and fretted:

There is a certain element lacking. It is the element which would hear this quartette if given at an opera or in a theater. What I want to know is why it is impossible to get this element which is really cultured and has good taste in regard to these things and which would hear good things in an opera— why it is impossible to get this element into a Methodist church? [19]

But his honest doubts were deeper than this might indicate, and he evidently tried to come to some compromise before abandoning the church entirely. An entry for October 28, 1894, shows the trend of his meditations:

The reverend Updike said . . . that a man who believed that right was right and wrong wrong: who believed that it was right to do right and wrong to do wrong—such a man though he doubted everything else might begin the Christian life. The sermon was on "What shall I do with my doubts?" And the gist of it was that he ought to lay his doubts on the shelf and cling to the things he believed. Use your positive belief, and let your negatives alone.

Becker could not let his negatives alone until he at least knew what they were, but he found that militant disbelief was every bit as uncongenial as bigoted Christianity. When he attended some of Robert Ingersoll's lectures on

[19] *Ibid.*, Oct. 25, 1894.

the Bible, he found much of the audience even less congenial than the usual Methodist congregations. "A man who disbelieves the Bible because most people believe it, makes me tired," he wrote. He concluded that "it is just as vulgar to be parading one's skepticism . . . as to be parading one's fanaticism." [20]

No further indications of Becker's religious struggles appear in his college journal, but some of his friends heard the rest of the story years later. When he finally decided that, whatever he was, he was no longer a Methodist, he wrote a letter to his pastor in Waterloo explaining his position and withdrawing his membership. In answer he received a scathing letter denouncing him as a renegade. This troubled him considerably for some time but did not induce him to rejoin the church. A few months later he abruptly and permanently ceased to worry about his unregenerate state when he learned that the clergyman who had castigated him so roundly had himself just eloped with the wife of a parishioner.

By that time Becker must have felt himself "preordained to contemplation and not to belief." All believers were "too noisy and obtrusive" [21]—those who believed in their own ability to explain the universe not less so than those who relied on an anthropomorphic God. For Becker the comfort of certainty was receding. He ultimately learned "to live at ease in a world that is full of unexplained phenomena," saying to those who insisted that he must either accept certain explanations or offer others: "Not at all. I did not make the universe, and feel

---

[20] *Ibid.*, Jan. 9, 1894 [i.e., 1895], and undated.

[21] Friedrich Nietzsche, *Beyond Good and Evil,* p. 92, cited by Becker (Notes, drawer 2).

under no compulsion to explain it." [22] Before he had finished college, Becker had given up one of the chief comforts vouchsafed to man. He chose to go on without it, not seeking any equivalent.

He did not lose faith in man-made miracles until a good deal later. In the midst of his doubtful reflections about the value of the church, this sweeping affirmation occurs: "Feed a starving man and he will desire to reform if he is wicked. Educate him and he will know how to do it." [23] To the young progressives of Becker's college days, such a belief appeared almost self-evident. Although Becker was to question these and other progressive axioms sooner than many others did, that would not be for some years yet, and even when he renounced them, he fitted his age in being far more unhappy over the loss of his illusions about man than over the loss of his belief in a Beneficent Providence.

If he had any other personal preoccupations during his college years, they are not detailed in his notebooks. There is a hint, no more, that he may have had a disappointment in love. A line reading "to the one in whom I see only virtues" is written on a page of his journal, opposite these six lines:

> First darkness. Then a friend then light.
> Then pleasure, Happiness and Joy.
> These came, and then
>
> She went away. Then pain again and night.
> Then questions; and the wish
> It had not been.[24]

[22] Becker, untitled MS on historical evidence.
[23] "Wild Thoughts Notebook," March 5, 1894.
[24] *Ibid.*, undated.

The verse is not identified, but whether his own or someone else's, it must have had a personal appeal for him.
Several cryptic remarks about women and about love
are scattered through the notebooks. For example: "It is
nearly as beautiful to see others make love as it is sad to
make love yourself." But whether he wrote these out of
vague and general adolescent melancholy or out of a particular unhappiness cannot be told (even in his private
notes he did not shed his reserve), nor does it matter.
One thing is sure: neither the lack of a definite voca-
tional aim, nor love, nor religious doubts stayed his intellectual development. Perhaps he learned early to
dissipate unhappiness and worry by work.

In 1896 Becker received his bachelor's degree. He had
won honors in history for his senior thesis on the national
nominating conventions. With Turner's approval he began the next fall upon his graduate work, taking a major
in history with Haskins and Turner and a minor in economics with Ely. On the question of his minor subject,
Becker evidently bowed to Turner's judgment that "the
old union between history and literature is now broken
in all the growing colleges" [25] and put aside his thought
of a minor in literature.

Becker spent two more years of intensive study at
Wisconsin, the first year on a scholarship and the second
on a fellowship won in competition, according to Turner,
"with some of the best graduate students we have
had." [26] During 1897–1898 he taught his first classes,
four hours a week in a freshman section of English his-

[25] Frederick J. Turner to Becker, July 3, 1896.
[26] Turner to President Seth Low, Columbia University, Feb.
23, 1898.

tory, and pursued his study of the national conventions as far as available materials permitted.

For his last year of graduate work Becker succeeded in getting a fellowship at Columbia University. This last year of full-time study (1898–1899) was a triumph and a pleasure for him. He was by then prepared by knowledge and experience as well as by temperament to make the most of all that came his way. He dug deeper into the history of political conventions, making use of the unlimited resources in and near New York City. In June, 1899 he was awarded the Tappan prize for the best work of the year in constitutional law.[27] Perhaps best of all, he learned to know and appreciate two great and very different historians: Herbert L. Osgood, then writing his monumental history of the American colonies; and James Harvey Robinson, soon to create a much larger stir with a much smaller book. When the year ended, Becker had to find a job. His forty-two years of teaching began in the fall of 1899 at Pennsylvania State College.

Becker tells us that at the age of eleven he made up his mind to be a writer. When he was twice that age, he decided that he would make a living teaching history while making a life writing it. Teaching he accepted as the price of a life of scholarship and writing, and he did not complain that the cost was too high, although it taxed his nervous energy exorbitantly. For the first ten years he taught, he had to screw up his courage anew every time he faced a class. If he later ceased to feel the strain so greatly, it was simply because he grew accustomed to it; he never learned to enjoy performing

[27] John William Burgess, undirected letter of recommendation, Aug. 30, 1899.

before an audience. As a young man he was quiet and shy, not of a "forthputting disposition," as Haskins recalled. Because this was so, neither Turner nor Haskins expected Becker to find teaching easy. They both officially expressed satisfaction with his handling of the freshmen sections at Madison,[28] but they both realized that his strength lay in his mastery of the written, not the spoken, word. Their affectionate anxiety on this point appears again and again in their letters. Turner wrote at the beginning of Becker's first year of teaching: "I know you will have a hard time of it this year, yet if you weather these seas, you will be a more experienced sailor and will *find* yourself." [29]

Becker weathered the seas well enough, at least, to send back cheerful reports of his progress. He remained two years at Pennsylvania State College and at the end of that time was undaunted enough to accept a one-year appointment at Dartmouth, although he was warned that "the Dartmouth boys are rather lively" and that he "might find the disciplinary side of the work less pleasant." [30]

A surer sign that he felt himself safely launched in his profession was his marriage in the summer of 1901 to Maude Hepworth Ranney, a young widow with a small daughter. Becker had met his future wife, the daughter of a New York physician, during the year he studied at Columbia. They had one son, born in 1910.

[28] Turner to Seth Low, Feb. 23, 1898; Haskins, undirected letter of recommendation, Aug. 7, 1899; Haskins to McMaster, March 7, 1899; Haskins to Seth Low, Feb. 23, 1898.

[29] Turner to Becker, Nov. 17, 1899.

[30] Haskins to Becker, June 14, 1901.

Carl Becker

After Becker accepted the Dartmouth job, Haskins tried even harder to prepare him for a rough time:

You will need to devote a good deal of attention to the matter of discipline of the *suaviter in modo* kind and to general effectiveness in the class-room. If you can hold the Dartmouth boys down well, it will be an excellent recommendation for any kind of teaching position.[31]

The year was got through somehow, but none of this was at all to Becker's taste; he was evidently pleased to exchange the lively Dartmouth boys for the soberer students of the Middle West the following year.[32] In the fall of 1902 Becker went to the University of Kansas at Lawrence, where he stayed until 1916. He continued to receive (and to need) advice about teaching. Haskins wrote in 1903, "I am glad your work goes so well from the student side. Take a hint from the remark about not looking at your class! I remember that as a defect at Madison. Look them fiercely in the eye!" [33] None of it changed Becker's ways much, apparently. He was at Kansas what he was later at Cornell—a good teacher for good students only. For the others he had too little verve, too remote and cool an air.

Becker's colorless public manner was a disadvantage, but largely a temporary one. Haskins advised him:

If you will let me say so, it strikes me in general that a man of a rather quiet and not forthputting disposition, such as you

[31] Haskins to Becker, June 22, 1901.

[32] Haskins to Becker, Oct. 27, 1902: "I appreciate how you feel regarding the Western students as compared with the average eastern undergraduate, particularly in one of the smaller colleges of the East, and I know you must enjoy getting back to them."

[33] Haskins to Becker, Jan. 4, 1903.

had when I saw something of you, is likely to attain his proper place in his profession by growing into an institution where he has been long enough to make himself felt, rather than by moving about very much. The "hustler" has the advantage in moving and impressing possible employers, but does not always wear and often gets into hot water.[34]

This advice was followed and the forecast was borne out: Becker wore well. Perhaps he was chagrined by the hustler as he had been in his student days, but he did not try to imitate him. He stayed at Kansas fourteen years —long enough to "make himself felt" and to reflect much credit on the university as well as himself by his writing.

Becker's first published article appeared in the *American Historical Review* in 1900 during his first year of teaching, and from that time until his death in 1945 there was never a year in which he failed to publish something—sometimes a little and sometimes a lot, but all of it done with the greatest care. His first articles grew out of the study of national nominating conventions which he began as a college senior and pursued through three years of graduate study. From this beginning he worked back to the early history of political parties in New York State.

Between 1901 and 1903 he published four articles on the colonial parties in New York. He was frequently urged by Turner and Haskins to "bring his work to a head," to put his material together and submit it as a thesis, so that he could take his doctor's degree. "It is easy to drift away from the degree, and it is often a real

[34] Haskins to Becker, Jan. 23, 1907, Cambridge, Mass. Becker had asked Haskins' advice about accepting an offer at Amherst.

help to have it," Haskins pointed out.[35] Becker was not drifting, but at his own deliberate pace he worked toward his doctor's degree, which he finally took in 1907. By then Haskins had been called to Harvard, but Turner was at Madison to examine Becker and to see his thesis through publication in the Wisconsin University Bulletin. The thesis, *The History of Political Parties in the Province of New York, 1760–1776*, although it is still the best work on the subject, has never been republished. What may be called a fictional abstract of it, "The Spirit of '76," [36] has become a classic among American historical essays and has often been anthologized.

During the time he was writing his thesis, Becker began writing unsigned book reviews for the *Nation*. From 1903 until about 1920 he reviewed a great many books in American and European history. In 1910 he published his first article in a popular magazine. It was also his first public statement of his beliefs about the nature of history: "Detachment and the Writing of History" he called it, and it was published by the *Atlantic Monthly*. Soon Becker was writing signed articles and book reviews for several national magazines, the *Unpopular Review, Dial,* and *Nation* most regularly. His output was never prolific, partly because he never learned how to review a book without reading it carefully or how to write anything without revising it many times.

Becker's steadily growing reputation brought him the usual academic reward: offers of other positions, promo-

[35] Haskins to Becker, Oct. 27, 1902.

[36] Pub. in *The Spirit of '76 and Other Essays,* by Carl Becker, J. M. Clark, and William E. Dodd (Washington: Robert Brookings Graduate School of Economics and Government, 1927).

tion at Kansas, and finally a call to an eastern university. He went first to the University of Minnesota, in 1916, but when Professor Charles Hull, at the meeting of The American Historical Association in December of that year invited him to join the faculty of Cornell University, he found the invitation irresistible.[37] In the summer of 1917, just fifty years, as it happened, after his parents had gone west from New York, Carl Becker went back to their native state. He lived the rest of his life in Ithaca.

He went to Cornell, he said in his charming address, "The Cornell Tradition," because he was offered "a good salary for doing as I pleased." Cornell at that time, with its "loose jointed administrative system," came as close to fitting Becker's definition of an ideal university as any he was likely to find—"University: a voluntary association of people, all of whom wish to learn, none of whom wishes to teach or to be taught." [38] Even Cornell was a long way from fitting that picture, but it was freer of administrative red tape than most other American universities. A university where nothing was required of the professor was just right for a professor who hated to require anything of his students. Becker was enchanted with the answer he received when he finally inquired "what the home work would be—how many hours and what courses I would be required to teach."

Professor Hull seemed mildly surprised at the question. "Why," he said, "I don't know that anything is *required* ex-

[37] Becker, "The Cornell Tradition: Freedom and Responsibility," *Cornell University: Founders and the Founding* (Ithaca, N.Y.: Cornell University Press, 1943), p. 197.

[38] Notes, drawer 2.

actly. It has been customary for the Professor of Modern History to give to the undergraduates a general survey course in modern history, and sometimes, if he deems it advisable, a more advanced course in some part of it in which he is especially interested, and in addition to supervise, to whatever extent may seem to him desirable, the work of such graduate students as may come to him. We had rather hoped that you would be disposed to do something of this sort, but I don't know that I can say anything specific in the way of courses is really *required*. We have assumed that whatever you found convenient and profitable to do would be sufficiently advantageous to the university and satisfactory to the students.[39]

And so Becker went to Cornell in 1917 and found himself believing more and more firmly in "the Cornell tradition which allows a maximum of freedom and relies so confidently upon the sense of personal responsibility for making a good use of it."

The graduate students who came to take his seminar found that he had no more intention of assigning their stint of work to them than Hull had of assigning Becker's to him. One of his first Cornell graduate students has described Becker's attitude:

I remember vaguely that once somebody asked Carl what he was expected to do, when it was due, how long his paper should be, etc. Carl sat and stared at him for several minutes . . . cleared his throat and said something to the effect that he was damned if he could answer that question. He assumed, he went on, that people took his seminar because they were interested. Well, if they were interested, they would get to work, and if they had something to report they would sooner or later report. He would suggest topics that he thought were interesting, but he never assigned anything to anybody.[40].

"The seminar" (which never had any other name) kept nearly the same informal character through the score of years Becker taught it. A student taking the course in the early '30's has left a vivid account of the way it operated:

The seminars in my day were hardly organized. When I first came back as a graduate student, and timidly asked whether I could take the seminar, and was told, "Yes, of course," and then asked, "What are we doing this year in the seminar?" Becker answered, "Well, if anyone has a paper to read, he reads it. If no one has a paper to read, we talk. If no one has anything to say, we go home." And that was exactly as it was. Sometimes we went home early. Sometimes we stayed late, and sat fascinated as Becker talked, and smoked Camel after Camel, and then as the hour got late, and the little office he then had on the East side of Goldwin Smith Hall got darker and darker, he often ran out of cigarettes, and fished in the big dish of stubs for the longer stubs and relit them, and talked on.[41]

In his undergraduate course, History 42, Becker was not so free to follow "the strong bent of his mind." Although he was inclined to believe salutary neglect the best policy for graduate students, and possibly for all good students, his conscience and his zealous young assistants forced him to do something in the way of

[40] Letter to Guy Stanton Ford, cited in his obituary notice of Becker, *American Philosophical Society Yearbook, 1945* (Philadelphia, 1946), p. 343. The writer of the letter is identified only as a "lifelong friend of Becker's," but it is apparently Leo Gershoy.

[41] Val Lorwin to David Hawke, April 10, 1950.

standard assignments and examinations for the undergraduates. A single mimeographed sheet was given to
each student at the end of each lecture. It contained a
cogent summary of the lecture in one paragraph, and a
bibliography on the topic divided into "required" and
"additional" readings. Becker commented freely on the
books he listed and many of his students cherish complete files of these sheets for several courses. Still the
whole long line of assistants continued to mourn that
the course was a snap, and most of them had a try at
"unsnapping" it. They did not get far because Becker
was never interested in disciplining the slackers. He was
not interested in them one way or another and on the
whole preferred to be amiable where unpleasantness
would do no good anyhow.

I am in the midst of reading papers for H-44—interrupted
by students who come in wanting to know what they can do
about "that final grade"—which turns out to have been 45
or something like that. It is hard to answer these people con-
vincingly, because obviously nothing is easier than to cross out
the number 45 and write 85. I always want to do it, because
it's easy to do and would make them happy. But some vestige
of a conscience prevents.[42]

Becker always believed every man must be his own
taskmaster both morally and intellectually (a distinction he might not have made). In this regard he found
support in the words of the Quaker, George Fox:

I heard some of the magistrates . . . say among themselves,
—if they had money enough, they would hire me to be their
minister. This was where they did not well understand us and

[42] Becker to Lorwin [Feb., 1934].

our principles. But, when I heard of it, I said it was time for
me to be gone, for if their eye was so much to me or any of us
they would not come to their own teacher [i.e. their con-
sciences]; for this thing (of hiring ministers) had spoiled many
by hindering them from improving their own talents, whereas
our labour is to bring every one to their own teacher in themselves.[43]

While still a student at Wisconsin, Becker had written,
"A man can reform himself but none can do it for
him." [44] As a professor he was convinced that men could
"become possessed of insight and judgment and understanding" only by learning, that no man could be *taught*
them, and that misapplied teaching simply destroyed
learning. That was why he had "an aversion to teaching
and teachers," or rather, as he explained later, "to misapplied teaching and to over-zealous teachers." [45] Learning, investigating ideas with others who were interested
in them, was his conception of his job. Teaching as a
technique for spoon-feeding (or force-feeding) reluctant
students on "pre-digested facts and ready-made ideas"
repelled him. Although he worked hard on his courses,
putting a great deal of study into each lecture, he had no
heart for being an efficient teacher. He had no wish to
stand in the way of anyone's "purchase of a degree"; in
fact he proposed, in a piece of Swiftian satire, that the
whole process be facilitated by awarding the degree as
soon as the student had paid his full tuition. Then all
those who were merely after the useful label could get

[43] "Passages from G. Fox, Diary, 267" (Notes, drawer 2). The
brackets are Becker's.

[44] "Wild Thoughts Notebook," March 5, 1894.

[45] "Learning and Teaching," *Cornell Contemporary*, II (Oct. 24,
1930), 13–14.

out from underfoot. Only those interested in learning would persist; there would be no external rewards and no requirements, and the administrative machinery could be dismantled. "The University could cease to be an institution partly commercial and partly penal, and become quite simply a place of learning." [46] Then perhaps students might be brought "to their own teacher in themselves."

Becker prepared in the broadest way to direct and stimulate younger learners, but the student had to furnish his own motive power in order to establish contact at all. If he came to Becker's class wanting to learn, he would; if what he really wanted was credit for the course with as little trouble as possible, he could get that too; but if he wanted entertainment or a store of useful knowledge without any mental effort, he was sure to be disappointed. Becker thought the punishments and artificial incentives to learning in the American university system were increasing but ought to diminish.

As for himself, he never became either a disciplinarian or a showman. Indeed, he never developed or, apparently, cared to acquire that degree of histrionic proficiency which is indispensable to the good lecturer. His former students agree that his lectures were beautifully coherent and thoughtful, but most of them add reluctantly that they were delivered in a low and monotonous voice, without any change of pace or dramatic high lights. None of these comments apply to his seminars, of course, but when the occasion demanded a fairly formal lecture, the lecturer himself was completely submerged. He organized what he wanted to say carefully, usually

[46] *Ibid.*, p. 14.

writing out his opening sentence in full, and outlining the rest of the lecture—in considerable detail in his early years of teaching, more sketchily later. He then delivered it in the most noncommittal fashion, declining to exploit his personality to put it across in any way. His words had to fend for themselves with no help from him. He attended to the thought and presented it as impersonally as a printed page, with seldom a gesture or an emphatic word. Those who came early, sat near the front of the classroom, and concentrated on what he was saying were well rewarded always, and sometimes were delighted by a "trick phrase or a twist of thought that was brilliant and fascinating." [47] The rest found the lectures hard to hear and dull.

In spite of that, his undergraduate course was fairly swamped with students from about 1924 until he retired in 1941. Before 1924 or thereabouts, History 42 usually had fifty to sixty students. Part of the great increase in the number of his students seems to have resulted from a piece of publicity given to the course by an enthusiastic student. Andrew J. Biemuller, later member of the House of Representatives from Wisconsin, took Becker's course while he was an enterprising reporter for the *Cornell Daily Sun,* and he wrote for it a glowing account of History 42 and of Cornell's eminent historian. The story had two lasting effects. It apparently began a vogue for taking Becker's course which soon doubled and then tripled the size of the class, making things uncomfortable for Becker, whose voice was quite inadequate for so large a group. It also provided a boner that Becker never ceased to enjoy: in the peroration of his article, Bie-

[47] Glen W. Gray to David Hawke, Feb. 9, 1950.

muller declared that Becker's course had "few equals and no peers" in the university.

Undoubtedly many students were disappointed to find that the famous historian had no glamour or sparkle on the lecture platform, but apparently a good many thoughtful students, quite aside from those who were interested in history for its own sake, found the undergraduate course in modern history rewarding and memorable.[48] Becker was aware that he was no orator; he was a writer and that was all he ever set up to be, although he did a good deal of lecturing outside the classroom in the last twenty years of his life. Reports indicate that he was more effective in his public lectures than he was in the classroom. This is partly explained by the fact that he insisted on using a loud-speaker system for public lectures. But he apparently had a livelier manner, too. Was it perhaps because he could be sure that he was not speaking to a captive audience? The sight of a roomful of young people who would obviously rather be somewhere else is sometimes enough to undermine much more confident speakers than Becker.

A photograph of a history group at Cornell taken in the early 1920's shows Becker as a smooth-shaven, stocky, youthful-looking man—rather square-jawed and weathered. Aside from his spectacles he had little of the look of the scholar and nothing of the esthete. He could still have passed for an up-and-coming Iowa farmer with his feet entirely on the ground. Despite his sturdy appearance, it was not long after this photograph was taken that he began having the painful gastric troubles that

[48] Many letters to Becker bear this out; for example, see Chauncey J. Gordon to Becker, June 23, 1932.

prostrated him again and again during the next twenty years. He underwent his first operation in 1924. For several months afterward he felt weary and apathetic about everything.

Partly to speed his recovery, he went abroad for the summer with a group of his colleagues. This was Becker's only trip to Europe. He was fifty-one years old. Although he enjoyed finding everything just as he had pictured it—in England especially—there was a bitter-sweetness in it all. "My foreign travel has come too late," he wrote to his wife. "I should have come to France at the age of 25. Then it would have been an experience of incalculable benefit." [49] There was nothing for it but to get what he could out of his belated tour, and this he did conscientiously. In France particularly it was more of an effort than a pleasure to see the places he thought he ought to see. Getting around without speaking the language was difficult, and Becker did not attempt to speak French in France. His pronunciation was strictly and deliberately American, even to sounding final consonants —Jean Paul Marat was "John Paul Mara*t*." This served very well for students taking notes in a class on the French Revolution. Although he did not repine, he always regretted that he did not go abroad until "late in life, when nothing could any longer be as glamorous as it should have been, and would have been in my youth." [50]

Although the trip made Becker nostalgic for the zest of his youth, perhaps it served its turn. His health improved greatly during the tranquil weeks he lived in a

[49] Becker to Maude Becker, Paris, Aug. 24, 1924.
[50] Becker to Elizabeth Bohannon, July 25, 1933.

small country hotel in Gloucestershire, although his cure proved to be only temporary. He remained subject to ulcers in spite of all the treatments and dreary diets that were prescribed and faithfully followed. He suffered one attack after another through the decade of the thirties. His friends grew accustomed to meeting at the bedside salons he held in his New York hospital room. Finally, in 1940, Becker submitted to a newly developed and very drastic operation, which effected a complete cure.

When, in 1941, Becker retired from active teaching, he was not sorry to have done with it, "but sorry only that I have reached the age when one is not sorry to be done with it." [51] Still he was convinced that, for him at least, "as rackets go, teaching and writing is one of the best." [52] Cornell had provided an unusually congenial home for Becker, spiritually and physically, for a quarter of a century. In spite of all enticements, he would never leave Ithaca except for temporary tours of duty, but he did accept summer appointments, lecture engagements, and research fellowships which took him all over the United States. He taught summers at the University of Michigan, the University of Chicago, Stanford, and Columbia. He lectured on special foundations at Yale (the Storrs Foundation, 1931), Stanford (the Raymond Fred West Memorial Foundation, 1935), the University of Virginia (the Page Barbour Foundation, 1940), and the University of Michigan (William W. Cook Foundation, 1944). When Becker had a term's leave from Cornell in 1935, he and his wife took a leisurely trip to California by ship through the Panama Canal. He spent a few weeks at the

[51] Becker to Max Lerner, May 7, 1941.
[52] Becker to Gottschalk, May 3, 1940 (files of Louis Gottschalk).

His Life

Huntington Library by special invitation and then went on to Stanford University, where he gave the West Memorial Lectures, which were later published under the title *Progress and Power.*

As it happened, the few years that remained to Becker after his retirement were among the most active of his life. His health, up to the week before he died, was better than it had been in years; that alone was a joy to a man who for ten years had been in hourly dread of another devastating illness. He wrote three more books after 1941, all notably more cheerful in tone if not fundamentally more optimistic than most of his writings in the preceding twenty years.

Upon his retirement from teaching, Becker had become Cornell Historian, a position whose duties he was left to define for himself in traditional Cornell fashion. He discovered only that "there is a general expectation that I will occupy myself somehow with the history of Cornell University" and he suspected that the job was "chiefly an excuse for giving me a reasonable pension." [53] At the same time he was invited to give the Messenger Lectures in 1942–1943, with the suggestion that he speak on some aspect of Cornell's history. He soon decided to devote the six lectures to the founding of Cornell University and "to relate it to the broad general subject of education so as to bring out the fact that the founding of Cornell was a significant aspect of the general trend in modern times toward history and science." [54] Out of this undertaking came *Cornell University: Founders and the Founding*, Becker's first book based on extended research

[53] Becker to Gottschalk, July 18, 1941 (Gottschalk files).
[54] *Ibid.*

in manuscript sources since his doctor's thesis. Becker evidently enjoyed the task, although some of his friends regretted his spending his time on so parochial a topic.

He spent the spring term of 1942 at Smith College as Neilson Research Professor, and for a few weeks in 1943 the war took him to Washington, where he helped to write a report for the United States Air Force. For the most part, however, Becker spent his last four years at home in Ithaca following much the same routine as usual —writing in the morning, tending to his personal affairs in the afternoon, relaxing with a long drive or a movie or a mystery story in the evening. After an illness of only a week, he died of uremic poisoning on April 10, 1945, at the age of seventy-one. Following the funeral services at Sage Chapel on April 13, his body was cremated and the ashes interred at the Pleasant Grove Cemetery in Ithaca.

Becker was committed by temperament and by conviction to the tragic view of life. A man of sanguine temper with a romantic sense of life would find Becker's philosophy pessimistic, skeptical, and chilling. He might, in spite of that, see that Becker's vision of man's history as high tragedy had an austere beauty of its own. Instructed by the new science of his generation, Becker saw what man's end must be:

Within a brief moment of eternal time the earth will grow cold, and all of man's alleged "imperishable monuments" and "immortal deeds" will be as if they had never been, nor will anything that then is be either better or worse because of anything that man has ever done or wished to do.[55]

[55] *Progress and Power* (2d ed.; New York: Knopf, 1949), pp. 114–115.

Building on this "firm foundation of unyielding despair," [56] he could, with Pascal, take peculiar pride in man's unique significance—"that he is insignificant and is aware of it." Man's best hopes will always be thwarted, and he will be crushed by the omnipotent universe:

Of all that, the universe knows nothing. Apart from man, the universe knows nothing at all—nothing of itself or of infinite spaces, nothing of man or of his frustrated aspirations, nothing of beginnings or endings, of progress or retrogression, of life or death, of good or evil fortune. The cosmic view of the universe of infinite spaces, and of man's ultimate fate within it, is man's achievement—the farthest point yet reached in the progressive expansion of human intelligence and power. It is not rightly to be taken as a description of events that are relevant to man's purposes, but rather as an ideal result of those purposes—the manifestation of his insatiable curiosity, his indefeasible determination to know. As such it is less an objective world of fact than man's creation of the world in his own image. It is in truth man's most ingenious invention, his supreme work of art. [57]

That one freedom which man does possess—the freedom to learn, to know—must be cherished, and above all used. "Man is a reed, but a thinking reed; all our dignity consists in thought. Endeavor then to think well; it is the only morality." These words of the Jansenist mystic, Pascal, became Becker's moral imperative.

But deeply as he valued reason, Becker never believed it was "the axis on which the world turns." [58] The life of

---

[56] Bertrand Russell, "A Free Man's Worship," *Mysticism and Logic* (London: Allen and Unwin, 1917), p. 48.

[57] *Progress and Power,* pp. 115–116.

[58] Hans Vaihinger, *The Philosophy of 'As If,'* trans. C. K. Ogden (London: Kegan Paul, 1924), p. 161. This is one of the books

reason was an ideal cherished by few and realized by none. Some sort of instinctive human decency had to be relied on in the main, Becker was sure. He worried because simple good will was becoming every day less adequate for making good citizens as we moved away from a simple frontier society into a complex world society. This became dramatically apparent during the Second World War, when ordinary "good" people hoarded sugar and tires and soap and bought steak on the black market. Becker wrote to Max Lerner that he thought that most people were "more or less all right . . . and will do what is necessary in so far as they can realize what we're up against." "But," he added, "most people—high or low—not having imagination can't really realize it." [59] He had indicated what, in his opinion, "all right" meant several years earlier when he had said about the English: "They're much the nicest people in Europe. They play the game better than anyone else. They're fundamentally honest and pessimistic (but not cynical) and deep down full of sentiment." [60]

They play the game—they do not except themselves from the rules which men have made to regulate their conduct with one another. But more than that, this remark really reveals Becker's beliefs about man in relation to the universe. He liked men who played the game in the cosmic sense as well: men who being "honest and pessimistic" saw that no creed, no human values had any

Becker said had most influenced his thinking "or at least clarified ideas I already had (which is about the only way books influence thinking anyway)" (Becker to the editor, *New Republic,* XCVII [Dec. 7, 1938], 135).

[59] Becker to Max Lerner, March 11, 1942.
[60] Becker to Elizabeth Bohannon, July 25, 1933.

sanction in the world of brute fact but who nevertheless went on behaving as if human ideals mattered in the universe, who went on abiding by rules which give form and beauty to life though its ultimate significance be naught. In this way man might preserve as "practical fictions" ideas which "perish as theoretical truths." [61] For instance, he may believe theoretically in rigid determinism, but he will live by the practical fiction of free will; he may see that society must hold sane men responsible for their actions, though they cannot help being as they are and doing what they do. Such unreal absolutes as free will, justice, and impartiality are as necessary to man in society as the mathematician's dimensionless points in geometry. Becker did not wish to destroy the illusions by which man lives nor to diminish their value, but he wanted to distinguish them from actualities. "One of the first duties of man is not to be duped, to be aware of his world." [62] He will have to act, if he is to act at all, on hypotheses, uncertainties, and downright fictions, but let him know what he is doing all the while he plays the game with a good heart.

This double consciousness does much to explain the enigma of Becker's character. He was both the observer on Olympus looking down at the activities of men (including his own),[63] and at the same time he was Carl Becker of 109 West Upland Road, a man "deep down full of sentiment"—head of a family, doting grandfather, teacher, voter, affectionate and loyal friend of other fallible human beings. As a cosmic critic Becker poked fun at the notion that man could attain detachment, but

[61] Vaihinger, *op. cit.*, p. 49.   [62] *Everyman*, p. 249.
[63] Cf. *Progress and Power*, pp. 19–20.

as a historian he himself exhibited what was, in human terms, vast detachment; he observed that human reason is fallacious, that it cannot answer ultimate questions, and that even where it does operate, "something deeper than reason determines our thought," [64] yet he maintained that "thought makes the whole dignity of man" and lived and advocated the life of reason; he raised fundamental questions about the nature of facts, yet he acted on the belief that the only hope of the future lay in "the extension of matter-of-fact knowledge"; [65] although he saw that science offers only "anesthesia in this life and annihilation in the next," [66] he yet declined to accept any more comforting form of truth.

There is no real contradiction here, nor any intent to be paradoxical. Becker was a spiritual descendant of David Hume, a true skeptic, "diffident of his philosophical doubts, as well as of his philosophical conviction." [67] He could not forbear philosophical speculation, but he did not expect it to provide him with a handbook of useful answers. Reflection seldom yielded new or wiser rules for playing the game, though it revealed many absurdities and delightful illogicalities in the old ones. A kind of wry awareness of one's own insignificance and one's own irrationality—an awareness which did not prevent action but did modify expectations—was the thing to aim at.

Through most of his life Becker had a greater horror of pretension and pomposity than he had of cynicism.

[64] Notes, drawer 2.   [65] *Progress and Power,* pp. 110–111.

[66] Notes, drawer 2.

[67] Hume, *Treatise of Human Nature:* Book I, "Of the Understanding," ed. T. H. Green and T. H. Grose (London: Longman's Green, 1882), I, 552.

Only after the rise of blatantly cynical dictatorships that denied humane values did Becker feel the need of affirming values. Until then he had been inclined to take good will for granted and to concentrate on the need for critical intelligence to guide it. His conception of morality as good thinking may appear to imply an insensitivity to the emotional needs of men, but one of his students says, "I have never known a man who so intuitively felt the problems and compromises all humans encounter and allowed for them with such comprehending sympathy." [68] One cannot examine Becker's personal papers without feeling this power of sympathetic imagination. It is evident in the warm, encouraging letters he wrote to his students and former students just when they needed them most, in his letters to his family and to old friends, and even in letters to strangers whose needs he felt. Always Becker was intensely sensitive to physical suffering. Years of illness and fruitless medical treatment brought him a bitter acquaintance with the pain and the nasty, brutish humiliations in the gift of nature. The deliberate bestiality of totalitarian regimes revolted him as nothing else could do.[69] His files show that he was deeply concerned over the plight of several European scholars who fled Nazi or Fascist rule and that he was prompt and tireless in writing letters in their behalf. He arranged introductions and lecture engagements for them; he helped them to obtain grants for research and study from various foundations and learned societies; he interceded when they had difficulties with the immigration authorities; he did what he could to find them teach-

[68] Geoffrey Bruun to David Hawke, Feb. 4, 1950.
[69] Conversation with Prof. F. G. Marcham.

ing positions. This was a task that was never finished in his lifetime, because many of the available jobs—especially for older men—were temporary, and the whole business of searching out openings and writing persuasive letters had to be done over and over again.

There is ample evidence in his private papers that Becker was unusually sensitive to other men's needs, but his ironic awareness of men's follies was more widely known. The statement that he was cold and aloof is often made and commonly accepted. This is not in accord with his private letters, but it was a natural enough judgment for a stranger to make in view of his reserve, his tendency to be silent and observant in social gatherings. Becker had not the buoyant temper nor the health and energy that enables some to enjoy any human contact and to find all men interesting. Often ill and tired, he was utterly bored by ordinary, respectable people, and could hardly abide pretentious ones. "The pessimist often becomes a misanthrope," writes Herbert Muller; "but he is also notoriously apt to be a more charitable fellow than the optimist who is in touch with the absolute, and who has therefore a laudable eagerness to share the truth, a reasonable impatience with those who fail to see it." [70] This puts one in mind of Becker, who, while he was not a misanthrope, must have seemed like one to a number of people. And he certainly was a charitable fellow, although he was never a "good mixer." Thinking that most people would rather talk than listen, he was inclined to let them, although at times he was lively, even sparkling, in conversation with a few people.

[70] Herbert J. Muller, *Modern Fiction* (New York: Funk & Wagnalls, 1937), p. 36.

His shy habits made people slow to discover that the coolness of his head did not proceed from coldness of heart. Even his department chairman at Kansas was distressed by Becker's shyness and suggested to Turner that he and Haskins might drop him a helpful hint about it:

You may perhaps be interested to hear of Becker. He seems to be getting on well with the students and I am well satisfied with him. He draws on his head much criticism from certain persons—Hodder particularly—on account of his appearance [of?] offishness, of which you have spoken before.[71]

A few years later Hodder was one of Becker's most intimate friends and remained so all his life.

Becker did not wear his heart on his sleeve; in fact he was inclined to be sardonic and self-deprecating about his own ideals and emotions. He often disclaimed any wish to "do good," having discovered after the golden days of the Progressive movement how naïve and officious reform could be.

I am one of those who are more interested in finding out so far as possible what men are like and how they think than in "doing them good," which I rationalize by saying that the way I can do them most good is to find out what they are like, what they do and why they think it's a good thing to do it.[72]

These remarks are not an exhibition of cynicism; they are an indication of a complex, self-critical intelligence determined to reduce ideals and ideas to their lowest terms. Only by so doing, he thought, could one guard against disillusion and romantic despair. If this be cyni-

[71] Abbott to Turner, March 9, 1903 (Wisconsin State Historical Society).

[72] Becker to Thomas Reed Powell, Dec. 3, 1944.

cism, perhaps a saving trace of it is needed to enable men who are both honest and sensitive to preserve their sanity.

Becker was deeply aware of the pitfalls of illusion. Disappointment engendered by over-optimism led him to lose his usual balance and growl at the universe in 1919–1920. He found the war of 1914–1918 "the most desolating and repulsive exhibition of human power and cruelty without compensating advantage that ever was on earth." [73] He was more disillusioned by the Peace of Versailles than by the war, but most of all he was disgusted by the obfuscation that accompanied the treaty debate in the United States. He was outraged by Wilson's inexplicable insistence that he had attained the settlement he had gone after. Becker concluded: "The man has no humor, no objectivity, no abiding sense of reality. . . . To say that the Peace conforms with the 14 points is either the result of dishonesty or an egoism that enables him to see black as white." [74]

Becker later admitted that he had no business being so bitter, that he had indulged in romantic hopes: "I had had a moment of optimism, had experienced a faint hope that Wilson might do what he wished to do. When he failed, I was angry because I had failed to see that he must fail; and took it out on Wilson." [75] Becker recovered

[73] Becker to William E. Dodd, June 17, 1920. (The original letters from Becker to Dodd are in the Dodd papers in the Library of Congress.)

[74] Becker to Dodd [ca. June 12, 1920].

[75] Becker to Dodd, Feb. 26, 1923. Becker forgave Wilson far too soon for the taste of some other liberals, who, like Oswald Garrison Villard, wanted to believe, and so believed, that when Wilson went to Paris, "the world was his to mold—if he dared" (editorial,

his equanimity by recapturing his long-range perspective; he reminded himself that he had no business with anger, which was for those who put up the barricades, not for the historian who wanted to understand the world. Becker did want to understand the world, not to change it—a sign surely of humility as well as of skepticism.

In any case, the kind of doing good that arises not from conviction about what is "good for people," but from affection and sensitivity, is quite another thing, and that was ingrained in his habits. When he was a child his family thought Carl particularly blessed in having inherited his mother's sweet disposition. However he came by it, his amiable temper was appreciated by all those who had dealings with him. Although he admitted to being "very cross-grained before he had his morning coffee," [76] although he was often moody and depressed, there remains not a single snappish letter or biting review to show for it. He never engaged in the academic quarrels that warm the columns of many a scholarly journal. Of course, people were occasionally offended by his reviews and fired off heated rebuttals to him, but it was Becker's habit to answer such letters courteously, with a disarming candor which usually restored men rapidly to their wiser selves, instead of provoking them further.[77]

Another family inheritance, apparently, was his habit

Nation, CXVI [Feb. 14, 1923], 166). Becker identified this editorial as Villard's in his letter to Dodd, Feb. 26 [1923].

[76] Becker to Dodd, June 17, 1920.

[77] See James Truslow Adams to Becker, Oct. 21 and Nov. 10, 1932; W. P. Garrison to Becker, Feb. 2 and Feb. 10, 1905; Becker to Combes de Lestrade, Oct. 15, 1900.

Carl Becker

of prompt and orderly dispatch of his affairs. Becker said
after his father's sudden death in 1919 that he "left his
affairs just as he would have done if he could have foreseen his death." [78] Carl Becker lived in the same fashion.
He generally answered his letters the day they were received and never failed to deliver manuscripts to his
publishers ahead of the time they were promised. Like
many men of complex and subtle minds, Becker lived a
simple life, achieving intellectual clarity by reflecting
deeply and persistently on a few central ideas through
which he approached all the problems of man.

[78] Becker to Dodd, Dec. 2, 1919.

II

Becker's Conclusions about History

I venture to say that our knowledge of historical facts, as well as the inferences drawn from the facts, is relative and not absolute. . . . If this leads to absolute skepticism then all I can say is that absolute skepticism is what it leads to.[1]

BECKER has been a highly controversial figure in the historians' guild not because of the history he wrote, but because of the questions he raised about the whole historical enterprise and because of the unsatisfactory answers he arrived at. Although he was by no means the first American historian to question the validity of the *Lehrbuch* rules for writing history, he probed more deeply into the matter than his predecessors had, came to more radical conclusions, and set forth his ideas more compellingly. He was uncommonly concerned all his life with the nature of historical knowledge and with the purpose of it. A number of American historians have tried to formulate a creed about their craft, but usually they have done it toward the end of their careers. Presidents of the American Historical Association often have

[1] Becker, "Commentary on Mandelbaum," MS, Becker Papers.

made some sort of statement in their presidential addresses of what they believed to be the historians' proper aims and appropriate methods, but many of them have not previously written anything on historiography—being always preoccupied with writing history instead. When they write their addresses, they view their own work and that of their contemporaries in retrospect—they note new tendencies which have appeared; they discuss what purposes have been served, which practices and principles have been fruitful, and which barren; and they describe the pattern, if any, that has seemed to them to emerge from man's history. Becker, on the other hand, was never fully absorbed in the pursuit of the facts, in the reconstruction of the past; he began searching for a philosophical basis for history at the beginning of his career. It was his nature to be always asking "why?" as well as "what?" Moreover the political atmosphere in his youth made him ask what was the historian's relation to society. Populism swept through the West, and the theme of social justice stirred American colleges and universities during the time Becker was growing up. The University of Wisconsin came to be particularly identified with the Progressive movement in the early twentieth century, but even before that—in Becker's student days—the liberal tradition of social service had prevailed in the School of Economics, History, and Political Science. Although Becker was not by temperament a reformer, his conscience was sensitive and he had at bottom a conviction "that knowledge and the power it confers should be employed for promoting the welfare of the many." [2] Just how this was

[2] *Cornell University*, p. 203.

best to be done was a problem Becker thought a good deal about, and one which set him early to puzzling about the nature of history. That his answer would lie in the direction of art rather than of science could have been predicted.

The object of this chapter is to show what answers Becker found to the question, "What is history?" This will be done by summarizing his more important essays and referring to other relevant papers. General analysis and criticism of his views will be reserved for the following chapter.

Becker once told a next-door neighbor, a professor of English, that he had decided to become a historian because he wanted to write and he was afraid he would find himself running out of anything to say midway in his career unless he learned something to write about as well as learned how to write.[3] If this was nine-tenths joke, the other tenth was an important aspect of the truth. His natural bent was toward literature, not science, and so toward history as a branch of humane letters. If his teachers had been of the opinion that history had nothing to do with literature, that it was a science pure and simple, that the historian could absolutely establish the facts and that doing so was his sole job—none of this would have made Becker a typical "scientific historian." It might, however, have kept him from becoming a historian at all. But he did not have any such mischance. Becker's description of his introduction to history in his essay on Frederick Jackson Turner is well known; an earlier reminiscence in a letter to Turner is even more emphatic on this point:

[3] Conversation with Prof. Walter French, Cornell University.

Carl Becker

It was in 1894 that I took my first course with you—that general course based upon the "Epoch Series." Until then, I had never been interested in history; since then, I have never ceased to be so. For this effect, I hold you entirely responsible, since it was not the subject but the teacher that interested me. The pack of enveloped notes which you brought to class influenced me more than the information contained in it. About the "facts" of history, I learned but little in that course. So far as I recall, I answered correctly only one question during the year, the answer was 1811, but the question I have forgotten. I think you gave us to understand that no one, not even Mr. Thwaites, knew "exactly what happened," that you did not yourself know, but to me at least you seemed mightily interested in selecting, from the infinite number of things that were said to have happened, things that had meaning and significance. Some of the ideas you threw out, often casually enough, may well have held fact and I found them to be keys that will unlock many doors. I do not remember whether South Carolina nullified the laws of the United States, but I learned that minorities are everywhere likely to be nullifiers; and the latter point offered up so much the larger field of speculation than the former, that I have never ceased considering it, and I think I have learned that where minorities can at best have only right on their side, majorities have generally fact on theirs, and invariably prevail in the end, which has puzzled me much, so that I have sometimes asked whether there is after all any difference between fact and right. I do not remember whether sovereignty resided with the state or with the nation in 1789; but I remember that you drew a diagram on the board to illustrate the problem, and that you said you hadn't a logical mind, which one ought to have if one wanted to be positive about such a question. I never forgot that remark and have since pondered, in a desultory way, the question of the logical and the historical mind, and have come to the conclusion that logic and history are two distinct ways (and perhaps the only ways) of apprehending reality, history being, however, the more comprehensive, since there is no logic of history but a very interesting history of logic. And then, you said once that it was all very well to poke fun at the philosophy of history, but that after all it was impossible not to have some kind of a Philosophy, the vital point being only whether one's philosophy amounted to anything. Another saying of yours, several times repeated, I remember: "History is the self-consciousness of humanity." That, at the time, meant absolutely nothing to me, but the saying must have been working all these years in the fringe of my consciousness, for I have recently hazarded in print the thesis that "we must have a past that is the product of all the present." This, I take it, is the same as saying that history is the self-consciousness of humanity. So you see you are responsible for what I publish, though, as they say in the prefaces, while quite agreeing to give you credit for the little good there may be in it, I do not hold you in any way liable for the much that is bad. I recall that you were interested in the Blue Ridge, and the Cumberland Gap, and the Old Cumberland Road, (or some such road). What it was you said, I do not remember: but I remember precisely the manner in which you said it. It was a manner that carried conviction—the manner of one who uttered great moral truths,—and somehow it has ever since stuck in my mind that the Blue Ridge, and the Cumberland Gap, and the Old Cumberland Road (or whatever road it was), are threads that will unravel the whole tangled skein of American history.

To me, nothing can be duller than historical facts, and nothing more interesting than the service they can be made to render in the effort to solve the everlasting riddle of human existence. It is from you, my dear Professor Turner, more than from anyone else, that I have learned to distinguish historical facts from their uses.[4]

[4] Becker to Turner, May 15, 1910 (draft).

Carl Becker

Seeing the impression Turner made on Becker, one would never guess that Turner had done his graduate work under Herbert Baxter Adams in the days when German doctrines were at their height at Johns Hopkins, but so he had. Turner did not deny that his interest was in ideas rather than facts. In answer to Becker's letter, which was one of many such testimonials Turner received when he left the University of Wisconsin, he said: "You especially have hit off in your letter what I would *wish* to accomplish. . . . You saw what I was more or less consciously groping after! And it's a pleasure to be understood in respect to one's ideals." [5]

None of the men who had much to do with Becker's education were ardent or unmodified "scientific historians." Haskins and Turner certainly were not, although they were ardent researchers and emphasized thorough training in the use of source materials. At Columbia Becker studied with Dunning and James Harvey Robinson, who both became notable critics of the claims and preoccupations of scientific history. He worked particularly with Osgood, but even Osgood was by no means an uncritical believer in the pure Von Ranke,[6] although he was distinctly no believer in literary history, feeling, according to his biographer, that "too much tooling of a phrase for great force or beauty would take time that should be given to finding out the truth." [7]

[5] Turner to Becker, June 24, 1910.

[6] Cf. Charles A. Beard, "That Noble Dream," *AHR,* XLI (Oct., 1935), 81.

[7] Dixon Ryan Fox, *Herbert Levi Osgood—An American Scholar* (New York: 1924), p. 115, quoted in *The Marcus W. Jernegan Essays in American Historiography,* ed. William T. Hutchinson (Chicago: University of Chicago Press, 1937), p. 287.

His Conclusions about History

As it happened, Becker's years at the University of Wisconsin coincided with the period of its great expansion in the new social sciences—a separate department of sociology was established in 1894–1895; a chair of psychology had been added to the philosophy department in 1888.[8] Economics and political science were strong and growing departments. Becker was not uninterested in these subjects, but his own inclinations were rather toward the humanities. Upon Turner's advice he chose economics for his minor field, but his own preference apparently was for literature as a minor.

Becker's doctoral dissertation is a fine example of the blend that may be made between scholarly requirements and literary ends. Although his study of the development of political parties in the province of New York contained a great deal of factual material, was heavily documented and based on wide and intensive research, Becker succeeded in mastering his material instead of letting it master him. He made of it a significant essay in the psychology of revolution. Taken as a monograph in local history it was an original contribution to knowledge, but it was also a comment on the way men think in times of political crisis. Even as a young man Becker was primarily interested in general ideas, not in the facts he had accumulated (though he had dug out a lot of new ones) but in the use of the facts to understand something about man, something that could never be proved but could only be imagined. Though Becker said that he was fascinated by the mechanics of research in his

[8] Merle Curti and Vernon Carstensen, *The University of Wisconsin, 1848–1925* (Madison: University of Wisconsin Press, 1949), I, 335.

youth,[9] his thesis indicates that he wanted, at least, to use what he found to build a structure of his own, however temporary it might be; he was not interested in "quarrying out of the bed-rock of historical fact" a few stones that might be used "in the permanent structure of some future master builder." In this preference Becker was out of step with his contemporaries who wanted above all, he thought, to make "a permanent contribution to knowledge," however small.[10]

As soon as he had demonstrated his ability to quarry good building stones out of the bedrock of historical fact, Becker launched an attack on the notion that this was the historian's only proper job. His specific target was the traditional set of rules by which scientific history was to be written, the rules which were to insure the historian against error and so assure the permanence of his contribution. He opened fire in 1910 in his first article to be published in a popular national magazine (*Atlantic Monthly*). He called it "Detachment and the Writing of History."

This article—Becker's first essay in historiography—foreshadowed all the future writing he did on the subject. It has not the aged, highly distilled flavor of "Everyman His Own Historian," but it is far from raw, and historically it is perhaps more interesting because it is one of the earliest and most extreme expressions of the relativist position in historical scholarship. Noting that historians did not yet seem to be disturbed by the questions pragmatist philosophers were raising about the

[9] "What Is Historiography?" *AHR*, XLIV (Oct., 1938), 20.
[10] "Detachment and the Writing of History," *Atlantic Monthly*, CVI (Oct., 1910), 525.

nature of truth itself, Becker said: "For them [the historians], certainly, truth is a fixed quality: the historical reality, the 'fact,' is a thing purely objective, that does not change; a thing, therefore, that can be established once for all beyond any peradventure." According to this view, if earlier historians had all been discredited, to some degree at least, by later findings, it was because they had worked unscientifically, telling their stories without first establishing all the facts. The modern historian had no doubt that he could at least establish facts which would stand forever, but he saw clearly the dangers of attempting to interpret his facts, of making a synthesis. Accordingly the more scientific he was, the stronger was his inclination to concentrate on the "hard facts" and to leave the job of making a synthesis for some future time after all the facts were in. It was this distinction between the facts of history and the synthesis which linked them into significance that Becker proposed to examine.

According to the methodologists, the historian should endeavor to record the facts objectively, and he could do this only by "cultivating mental detachment," becoming as nearly as possible like Nietzsche's "objective man" —a mirror to reflect whatever came before him—in this case historical facts. This brought Becker at once to the heart of the matter—what is the historical fact? And Becker gave his answer, the answer that he explored and developed for the rest of his life but never essentially changed:

It has come to a pass where the historical facts seem almost material, . . . something that can be handed about and pressed with the thumb to test its solidity. But, in truth, the

Carl Becker

historical fact is a thing wonderfully elusive after all, very difficult to fix, almost impossible to distinguish from "theory," to which it is commonly supposed to be so completely antithetical.

To illustrate his meaning Becker gave as an example of a well established fact: "Caesar was stabbed by the Senators in the Senate house at Rome." Then he demonstrated that this is actually a complex of numberless simpler facts:

Thus while we speak of historical facts as if they were pebbles to be gathered in a cup, there is in truth no unit fact in history. . . .

The historical reality is continuous, and infinitely complex and the cold hard facts into which it is said to be analyzed are not concrete portions of the reality, but only aspects of it. The reality of history has forever disappeared, and the 'facts' of history whatever they once were, are only mental images or pictures which the historian makes in order to comprehend it.

Becker based his conception of history upon the premises here given: first, that there are no discrete facts in history, no historical elements, every fact is a compound of smaller facts; second, historical facts are not solid substances which can be captured and examined; they are images present in someone's mind.

The implications of these two ideas are sweeping, and Becker pursued them tenaciously for years, as it was his pleasure to do with any idea that interested him. It was his notion that every idea was "a handle to every other idea," and his way of thinking was to start with one striking idea and patiently unravel its connections one by one. This habit made it possible for him to reduce the most complicated ideas to their simplest terms. He worked somewhat like a mathematician who cannot remember the formulas but always has to derive them for himself. In "Detachment and the Writing of History," he outlined in its most radical terms what he was to say in greater detail about the epistemological problem of history through the rest of his life.

Taking up the second point, that historical facts are mental images of past events, he asks how such images are created. He concludes that the statements about past events which the historian reads become images for him only if his own past experiences infuse the words with meaning. The particular image that comes to mind will owe much to the personal experience of the historian. If he knows nothing at all of the ancient world, for instance, when he first reads that Caesar was stabbed in the senate house he may see a room like the senate chamber in Washington with all the senators in frock coats. As he reads further he will get more information— he will learn that Romans did not wear frock coats, for example—and gradually the picture in his mind will change, but no matter how thorough his researches may be, "the facts of history do not exist for any historian until he creates them, and into every fact that he creates some part of his individual experience must enter."

The relationship Becker saw between the historian and his facts calls to mind at once Immanuel Kant's dictum about the experiencer and the world he experiences: "The mind is the law giver of nature." Man cannot ever experience the raw material of nature itself (the "noumena") but only nature conditioned by our means of perception (the "phenomena"). So the historian cannot

Carl Becker

see the historical reality but only images called up in his own mind. Just as the very quality of the human mind determines what we can experience in the present world of nature, so the limitations of the historian—his location in the here and now, his memory of certain experiences, his possession of certain concepts, his lack of others— prevent him from dealing with historical reality and confine him to dealing with mental pictures of it, more or less vivid and detailed.

Becker also reminds us that the experience of the historian is more than the lawgiver of his own images—it is the judge of their truth as well. "Experience not only furnishes the elements for the image which the sources guide us in forming: it is also the final court of appeal in evaluating the sources themselves." Few modern historians, for example, will believe tales of miraculous happenings, no matter how many witnesses swear to them, because in their experience such things do not happen in this universe.

One obvious conclusion emerges from this: if historical facts are images containing as a necessary ingredient part of the historian's own experience, then the "objective man, so detached and indifferent with no mental reservations referring to human affairs" would not, if he existed, be able to determine facts. By withholding himself entirely from his material he would be dooming it to remain meaningless, never to be precipitated into useful images.

Returning to his first point—that there is no unit fact in history—Becker draws the conclusion that every fact is in truth a synthesis, a combination in the historian's mind of other facts, each further divisible in turn.

His Conclusions about History

Strictly speaking, analysis and synthesis cannot be rigidly distinguished. And the reason is not far to seek: it is because there is no real analysis and no real synthesis. When the historian is engaged in what the methodologists call analysis, it is not the reality that he takes apart, but only the sources,—a very different matter.

Becker looks finally at the way historians actually operate when they are analyzing and synthesizing their sources. First, they break down each source into all the statements it contains and put them down on separate slips. When this is done and the historian has his case full of cards, then comes the problem of synthesis, which is "not to record exactly what happened, but by simplification to convey an intelligible meaning of what happened."

The problem of simplification is a problem of selection, and there's the rub. Even historians who had perfect faith in their ability to record facts objectively were daunted by the problem of objectively choosing a few among them to use in their narratives. Other social scientists had developed methods at least superficially like those of the natural scientists. They classified phenomena of human behavior somewhat as the zoologist classified sea shells—in terms of common qualities—but this was not a method of much use to historians, who are interested in telling about particular persons and particular events. What historians needed was an objective standard for determining the relative value of facts. And now (here he comes to his specific target) it seemed there was such a standard, "and one residing in the facts themselves, and therefore purely objective."

This new formula for solving the problem of historical

synthesis was the work of the German philosopher, Hein-
rich Rickert, introduced to American historians by Fred
Morrow Fling in 1903. For constructing the "historical
concept," the historian, according to Rickert (via Fling),
has only to look for four characteristics: "He must seek
facts that are unique, facts that have value on account of
their uniqueness, facts that are causally connected, facts
that reveal unique change or evolution." [11]

If historians proceed scientifically, they can determine
the relative value of the facts so clearly that "the same
facts will be selected 'by the opponents of the French
Revolution . . . as have been selected by the supporters
of it.' " [12] So also Catholic historians and Protestant historians should be able to agree on the importance of
Luther's role in the Reformation.

But that word "value" (speaking of the relative value
of facts) is disquieting, says Becker, despite Professor
Fling's urgent insistence that "the question of value is not
a question of partisanship, nor of approval or disapproval;
it is a question of importance." Becker still asks, "Important for what?" The answer "important for the Reformation" takes us back to the very concept which the
historian is trying to form scientifically. "All that we know,
therefore, is that the concept is formed by selecting the
facts that are important for the concept. . . . After all
do the facts come first and determine the concept, or does
the concept come first and determine the facts." The case
for the scientific historian is quite gone when it is virtually admitted that the concept comes first: " 'We know

[11] Fred Morrow Fling, "Historical Synthesis," *AHR*, IX (Oct.,
1903), 1–22.

[12] Becker, *Atlantic Monthly*, CVI, 531.

what the end was' and we wish to know the chain of events leading up to it," Fling says. Becker questions the sense in which we "know" what the end was—of the French Revolution, for example—and concludes that "unfortunately, the historian and his concepts are a part of the very process he would interpret." The historian's concept of the end of any important social process will depend upon the age in which he lives because "there is, in every age, a certain response in the world of thought to dominant social forces." Whatever the modern historian might be detached from, "certainly it is not from the dominant ideas of his own age."

To clinch his argument Becker turns finally to an examination of the historian at work—on the Protestant Reformation, for instance. Does he sit "thumbing his cards," deciding to use or omit each one on the basis of Rickert's four-point formula?

No such thing. As he goes over his cards, some aspects of the reality recorded there interest him more, others less; some are retained, others forgotten; . . . some facts strike the mind as suggestive . . . *because they associate themselves with ideas already in the mind.* . . . The original concepts, which give character to the entire synthesis, were contributed, not by the facts of the sixteenth century, but by the facts of the twentieth century.

If the historian has few ideas to act as "centers of attraction for new ideas," he is unfortunate indeed, for in scholarship as in the market place to them that hath it shall be given.

Instead of "sticking to the facts," the facts stick to him, if he has any ideas to attract them, and they will stick to him to some purpose only if his ideas are many, vivid and fruitful. Complete detachment would produce few histories, and none worthwhile; for the really detached mind is a dead mind, ly-ing among the facts of history like unmagnetized steel among iron-filings, no synthesis ever resulting in one case or the other to the end of time.

And so it was Becker's conclusion that a scientific formula for historical synthesis was neither possible nor necessary; that the old-fashioned, unscientific histories probably served a useful purpose—"and if useful and necessary, then true—true in the only way that historical synthesis is ever likely to be true, true relatively to the needs of the age which fashioned it." As for the idea of detachment—perhaps it would soon cease to be fashion-able and history might then get more interesting as it got less scientific. However scrupulous the historian may be, his tale is not and can never be absolutely true; it is only relatively true, true relatively to the needs of the age. Here was a downright statement of historical rela-tivism, one of the first to be made in this country.

Becker's unorthodox views did not blight his career. So far as his correspondence file indicates, his sally was wel-comed by the guild—no historian apparently recogniz-ing himself in Becker's portrait of the orthodox historian. Even Fred Morrow Fling, whose uncritical presentation of Rickert's views had called forth Becker's article, con-fessed to finding it interesting and entertaining; perhaps he did not find it shocking because he did not under-stand its implications.[13]

[13] Fling to Becker, Oct. 4, 1910: "I don't think I have any issue to take with your article concerning the difficulties of making a synthesis due to environment and personality nor touching the

His Conclusions about History

William A. Dunning wrote about the article, "You . . . said there lots of things that I believe to be profoundly true." [14] Probably the balanced judgment of Haskins, however, more nearly expressed the general opinion of American historians:

With most of the article I find myself in agreement and should be disposed to criticize matters of omission rather than commission. You are quite right that there is no such thing as absolute detachment, but that is no reason why, in most kinds of work, the greatest possible amount of detachment should not be striven for. In the last analysis it is also true that the synthetic and analytic operations cannot be distinguished; practically, however, there is a real distinction, and it is particularly on the analytic side that the element of detachment is most possible. Synthesis is inevitably more subjective. I realize, however, that your immediate business was rather to puncture certain prevalent misconceptions than to discuss how much practical truth might be left in them, and I congratulate you on the skill with which you have done it. [15]

Haskins' estimate of Becker's intention was a just one. The "Detachment" essay is the most provocative state-

---

process." He does not seem to see that Becker was saying that without "environment and personality" the historian would not be able to make a synthesis at all! A letter of two years later indicates even better the gap between them. Fling to Becker, May 22, 1913: "One amusing thing about it was the discussion of my attitude toward the marquis and marquise and the assertion that my sympathies were with the marquis. Quite the reverse being true, it would seem that I was fairly successful in maintaining an objective attitude toward him." The assumption that leaning over backward to conceal bias equaled objectivity was one that Becker lampooned sharply.

[14] Dunning to Becker, March 7, 1911.
[15] Haskins to Becker, Oct. 18, 1910.

ment of his view of historical truth that he ever published; it marks the upper limit of his relativism. It also was the high-water mark of his progressivism. A discontent with the life of thought, an impulse to action peeps out from between characteristic lines of graceful irony:

The state of mind best calculated to find out exactly what happened is perhaps incompatible with a disposition to care greatly what it is that happened; and whatever value the notion of detachment may have just now, the time may come —there have been such times in the past—when it is important that everyone should care greatly what happens. In that case, one can hardly think of the "objective man" as possessing qualities exceptionally well adapted for survival.[16]

If one had only this to go by, it might be legitimate to say, as someone has said recently, that Becker "saw the historian as a practical reformer." [17] But Becker saw the historian as a reformer only for a moment if at all. He no doubt did think that the day might come when it would be important for everyone to care greatly what happened (he may even have thought that the time was now) and that those historians who cared enough to help determine what should happen would more likely survive than those who just wanted to know exactly what it was that had happened, but still he could no more identify himself with one group than the other. A devastating critic of the notion that the past should be studied for its own sake he could be; but a dedicated believer in "exploiting the past in the interest of advance" he could not be. That much was evident no later than 1912 when he reviewed

[16] *Atlantic Monthly,* CVI, 536.

[17] Cushing Strout, "Historical Thought in America," *Virginia Quarterly Review,* XXVIII (Spring, 1952), 255.

His Conclusions about History

James Harvey Robinson's *The New History*. The review was friendly and appreciative as befitted an admiring former student of Robinson. Yet for all that, the one point on which he took issue with Robinson was far more telling than all the indignation poured out by such reviewers as Fred Morrow Fling, who disliked the whole business of New History.[18] When Becker found himself actually challenged by Robinson's words to renounce old ways and to write history which should be "a weapon" in the hands of the radical in his fight for progress,[19] he pulled up short and blurted out the difficulty—a profound one, which would serve to keep him from ever carrying out the doctrine he had seemed to advocate:

What, after all, is progress? What is the test, the standard of value, which is to determine the direction of conscious effort toward social reconstruction? Professor Robinson's only reply to this question is that "no one who realizes the relative barbarism of our whole civilization . . . will have the patience to formulate any definition of progress when the most bewildering opportunities for social betterment summon us on every side." This is very well if it is only a matter of doing what our hands find to do: one may venture to feed the starving before formulating a definition of progress. But if one wishes to remove the causes of poverty, a definition of progress might prove most useful. And certainly if the historian is to renounce his present aims and methods, and to set himself the task of "exploiting the past in the interest of advance," he needs a far more definite notion of what advance is than can be found in the statement "the most bewildering op-

[18] Fling, *Yale Review*, n.s., II (Oct., 1912), 166.
[19] Robinson, *The New History* (New York: Macmillan, 1912), p. 252.

portunities for betterment summon us on every side;" he needs in fact a genuinely scientific definition of progress.[20]

In spite of his skepticism about the New History, Becker was known for a critic of the Old, Past-for-its-own-sake History, and so he was invited to read a paper at the 1912 meeting of the American Sociological Society —an organization identified with the reform movement.[21] The over-all topic of the meeting was "The conception of human inter-relationships as a variant of social theory." The papers were to a large degree progress reports on how various social sciences (including psychology, education, and religion, as well as history, sociology, political science, and economics) were being set to work in the aid of social betterment.

Becker's paper was called "Some Aspects of the Influence of Social Problems and Ideas upon the Study and Writing of History." [22] The long academic title was probably not of his choosing, but it fits the article, which is rather an account of the history and development of current philosophies of history than a statement of Becker's own convictions or a witty attack on ideas not his own. This fits the plan of the meeting well enough—still the paper is out of key with the rest of the volume because Becker was unable to make the same assumptions about history that the other writers made about their disciplines. Becker could not speak with conviction about applying the science of history to the solution of social problems

[20] Becker, review of Robinson, *The New History, Dial,* LIII (July 1, 1912), 21.

[21] Its first president was Lester Frank Ward. Other leading members were E. A. Ross, Albion Small, and Jane Addams.

[22] Pub. in American Sociological Society, *Publications,* VII (June, 1913), 73–107.

when he did not think history was a science. Where other speakers did not doubt that soon "the searchlight of social science . . . would dispel much of the haze" [23] that surrounds the central problems of life, Becker, knowing that history was no searchlight, seemed to fear that it was more like a handful of matches—most of them damp. The few that would light might well, he thought, be used to illuminate the present, but no amount of them would make the kind of beam that burns away fog.

(Becker's paper is fundamentally a history of the rise and fall of the ideal of scientific history.) In a rapid survey of the nineteenth century Becker indicated that the historical writing of the first half of the century reflected faithfully the preoccupation of the age with political problems left unsettled by the French Revolution. Historic rights and gradual evolution of institutions were emphasized, not natural law and revolution. Between 1850 and 1875 a broader concept of history emerged, coming out of "the growing complexity of social problems." During the third quarter of the nineteenth century a change appeared in the methods as well as the subject matter of history. Because of the rising influence of natural science and because of the acceptance of Ranke's critical methods of research, history became "scientific." Scientific history came to imply also "a particular point of view in respect to interpretation." It came to mean the assumption of "the objective and detached attitude of mind with which the scientist regarded natural phenomena." To write scientific history it was necessary to renounce philosophy and eliminate all thought about the

[23] Albion Small, "The Present Outlook of Social Science," *ibid.*, p. 34.

present. But, after all, this style of history in its determined disregard of all save "the facts" fitted its age too:

This attitude of objectivity—the thorough-going renunciation
of the present, the disposition to reconstruct the past as a
whole, to know it for itself alone, to "justify that which is just
by the judgment of experience"—undoubtedly this attitude
was well suited to the spirit of the two decades after 1870. The
resplendent vision of Perfectibility, vouchsafed to the generous minds of the eighteenth century, was dimmed after 1815,
and again after 1848. In the sixties, the evolutionary philosophy fell like a cold douche upon the belief in progress
through conscious effort. The theory that man is one with
Nature was an old one, but the work of Darwin seemed to
furnish a positive demonstration of theories which had hitherto
rested on a purely speculative foundation. The biological law
of evolution, especially as applied to society by Spencer, indicated that progress, if there was such a thing, could come
only through the operation of mechanical forces. Man himself, at best hardly more than a speck of sentient dust, a
chance deposit on the surface of the world, might observe
the laws of development, but could neither modify nor control them. Materialism had its day in science, pessimism in
philosophy, naturalism in literature; religion seemed a spent
force. When all the old foundations were crumbling, historians
held firmly to the belief that facts at least could not be denied;
and in these days of acrid controversy, the past studied for
itself, as a record of facts which undoubtedly happened, was
a kind of neutral ground, an excellent refuge for those who
wished to sit tight and let the event decide.[24]

But again the atmosphere was changing. Men once
again were stirred by a conviction that man could improve his lot, and so they were demanding "that knowl-

[24] American Sociological Society, *Publications*, VII, 95.

edge shall serve purpose, and learning be applied to the solution of the problem of human life." For historians this meant asking of the past questions that had meaning for the present, and so abandoning the "scientific" ideal. This, Becker thought, was happening "though very slowly indeed." In the vanguard was James Harvey Robinson declaring that it was time for the present to "turn on the past and exploit it in the interest of advance." If few were willing to say so much, many were "ready to welcome new methods of interpretation which promise to bring our knowledge of the past to bear more directly and more effectively on the present than the prevailing method has been able to do." The real question in the air which interested Becker was how to know what was advance.

The importance of the fact can no longer be measured by the fact itself; it must, on the contrary, be judged by some standard of value derived from a conception of what it is that constitutes social progress—some tentative hypothesis, or conception of moral quality, or present practical purpose.

Looking around him Becker found among historians some "disposition to set up such standards for purposes of interpretation." One method, followed by a few historians, was "to seek in the remote past situations analogous to those of the present" and by studying them to throw light upon the future.

Another way of choosing the important historical facts was simply to treat the recent past far more fully than earlier periods and to emphasize those issues and events which still seemed important to us. Turner had expressed his belief in this method of studying the past in his presidential address in 1910 when he called upon history to "hold the lamp for conservative reform."

A far more controversial method of separating the important from the unimportant facts was to "bring them to the test of some conception of moral quality," but David J. Hill seemed to advocate such a method, and Henry Osborn Taylor said in 1911 that the historian must judge between good and bad.

But none of these practical methods was a complete or a new answer to the problem of synthesis. The first thoroughly philosophic answer to the question facing the new historians was that of Lamprecht. Becker confessed misgivings about his own understanding of Lamprecht, but attempted to describe his method, which depended "very largely upon psychology." Lamprecht maintained that the connection between all facts was subjective. He saw "the concrete events, the particular activities, as results of the psychological forces which are generated by social life." He abstracted from the concrete events the "social-psyche" which forms the underlying connection between all the seeming disconnected activities of a social group—between the painting of a picture and the passage of a bill in the legislature, for example. The social soul gradually changes as it is transmitted from generation to generation, and it is this cumulative social-psyche that impels men "to act as they do act." "The continuity of history is thus subjective," as Becker understood Lamprecht. "Its real substance is social experience deposited in nerve centers." The historian's job then is to interpret "the series of objective events in terms of psychic development."

Becker was obviously much interested in Lamprecht's

method but he saw that its scientific validity depended on the ability of psychology "to say whether there is a soul of society, to define the concept with as much precision as possible, to determine the process by which it operates and to formulate methods for detecting and measuring its influence." That would be no easy task.

In concluding his survey of the way social problems were influencing the study of history, Becker declined "to pronounce upon the legitimacy of any of the new methods," but he noted that they were likely to be used more and more. One of the critics of Becker's paper, a sociologist, was ready then and there to pronounce Lamprecht's methods thoroughly illegitimate, "a delusive philosophy of history which is neither sound philosophy nor trustworthy history." Contending that Lamprecht had "left the objective world of science" and "plunged into subjectivism," he insisted that valid historical interpretation "must, like the facts, be objective in reference and expression," and demanded from historians "a convincing interpretive method." [25]

In his brief answer to questions raised in the discussion of his paper, Becker made no attempt to answer these deeper questions, but he said in reference to Lamprecht:

It is quite possible to deal with the various sorts of particular activities in any period—the political, economic, religious, and intellectual activities—as illustrating, or as related to, certain mental or psychic characteristics common to the social group or nation. These common characteristics thus become a unifying principle round which facts or events, political or other, may be grouped.[26]

[25] A. J. Todd, *ibid.*, p. 112.   [26] Becker, *ibid.*, p. 112.

Such an approach could hardly fulfill Lamprecht's aim "to explain . . . in a severely scientific manner, exactly how the present is the product of the past." Becker saw in Lamprecht a fruitful suggestion, not a scientific method. One of Becker's most successful books—*The Eve of the Revolution*—perhaps owed something to this suggestion.

The anomalous meaning of the word "science" is forcefully exhibited in this volume of The American Sociological Society *Publications*. Becker and most present-day historians apply the term "scientific history" to history based on critical methods of research, *and* written with the sole object of telling "what really happened" without reference to modern man and his needs and interests. "Scientific historians" in that sense were not concerned with the uses of the past for contemporary society. Other social scientists, however, and some historians (notably Frederick J. Teggart) do not identify science with detachment from social problems. They wish to become more scientific in order to solve problems more efficiently. Accordingly, most of the papers given at this 1912 meeting cheered the rise of scientific study of society because it was yielding answers. Becker, on the other hand, cheered the decline of the scientific ideal in history because it had prevented historians from asking any of the right questions.

Becker's interest in the problem of synthesis remained keen. Brief comments scattered through his book reviews show this, but he did not again express his ideas on the subject at any length until fourteen years later, in 1926, and then only in a speech which he never published.

Before we examine this highly controversial speech, it

is worth while to take a look at Becker's review of H. G. Wells's *Outline of History,* written in 1921. Becker's remarks in the course of this review about the historical enterprise in general show clearly that the mood that had possessed him during the great progressive era was past and done with. He had grown older, wiser, wearier. He no longer asks for a definition of advance or for the setting up of standards of value by which the importance of historical facts can be judged. If he had ever hoped science could progress so far in the ethical and political realm (and there is little to show that he had) he seems to have given it up before 1921. The standards by which facts were judged interesting and important were, and would remain, relative to the times and the person judging them:

There is nothing one cannot find in the past—except the truth: a truth you can indeed find; any number of truths are there ready to be picked out. . . . In periods of stress, when the times are thought to be out of joint, those who are dissatisfied with the present are likely to be dissatisfied with the past also. At such times historians, those of the younger generation at least, catching the spirit of unrest, will be disposed to cross-examine the past in order to find out why it did not usher in a better state of affairs, will be disposed as it were, to sit in judgment on what was formerly done, approving or disapproving in the light of present discontents. The past is a kind of screen upon which each generation projects its vision of the future; and so long as hope springs in the human breast, the "new history" will be a recurring phenomenon.[27]

[27] "Mr. Wells and the New History," *Everyman,* pp. 169–170. This article was first published by the *American Historical Review,* XXVI (July, 1921).

Carl Becker

The conflict between the orthodox scientific view of history and the pragmatic or relativist view was fully under way by 1926. When the American Historical Association met in December at Rochester, New York, the general session of the first afternoon was given over to a discussion of the historian's data and method. Becker followed F. M. Fling's opening paper with a rousing presentation of the relativist view, asking "What is the historical fact?" Although the paper has never been published, it has still not been forgotten. Harry Elmer Barnes insisted ten years later (urging Becker to publish the paper) that it was, in his opinion, "the most important theoretical contribution to historical criticism since the days of von Ranke," that "it might well come to occupy the same position in historical science that the New Physics does in natural science." [28] Becker always maintained, however, that the paper was written "to provoke discussion" and did not accurately represent his considered opinions. It must have fulfilled its purpose amply, although the discreet reporter of the session in the *American Historical Review* gives a perfectly bland and colorless summary of Becker's remarks,[29] and there was no time for discussion during the meeting itself because Fling's paper ran far overtime.

By assailing the certainty of facts themselves, Becker was shaking the very foundation stone of orthodox methodology, perhaps of any methodology. To attack standard tests for establishing facts, to criticize the ways in which the facts were used, and to suggest new methods of combining and selecting facts were old and

[28] Harry Elmer Barnes to Becker, March 21, 1936.
[29] *AHR,* XXXII (Jan., 1927), 438.

His Conclusions about History

respectable undertakings. But Becker suggested that the raw material itself is no more concrete than the pattern which the historian weaves them into. All was subjective. Actually Becker said nothing in this talk which he had not at least implied in "Detachment and the Writing of History," but here he pursued to a logical extreme a few of the ideas in the earlier essay. He asked three questions at the outset:

1. What is the historical fact?
2. Where is the historical fact?
3. When is the historical fact?

To these questions he suggested "provisional" answers. To (1) he answered:

The historian may be interested in anything that has to do with the life of man in the past—any act or event, any emotion which men have expressed, any idea, true or false, which they have entertained. Very well, the historian is interested in some event of this sort. Yet he cannot deal directly with this event at all, since the event has disappeared. What he can deal with directly is a *statement about the event*. He deals in short not with the event, but with a statement which affirms *the fact that the event occurred*. When we really get down to the hard facts, what the historian is always dealing with is an affirmation—an affirmation of the fact that something is true. There is thus a distinction between the ephemeral event which disappears, and the affirmation about the event which persists. For all practical purposes it is the affirmation about the event that constitutes for us the historical fact. If so the historical fact is not the present event, but a symbol which enables us to recreate it imaginatively.[30]

[30] Becker, "What Are Historical Facts?" MS, Becker Papers. The title in some drafts is "What Is the Historical Fact?"

Simply then, the historical fact is an affirmation that something about an event is true. Where is it?

(2) "In someone's mind or it is nowhere." To those who protest that facts are "in the records, in the sources," Becker admits they are, in a sense, but adds if they are *only* in the sources, "lying inert" they are "dead facts," not even known to have been alive, "incapable of making a difference in the world." To those who would protest that the *event* itself has made a difference in the world even if no one now remembers it, Becker answers that this is true only because after the actual event people *did* remember it. Even an event like the assassination of Lincoln would not have made any lasting difference in the world if it had been forgotten immediately, if human beings, like dogs, did not possess enduring memories. "It is the persisting historical fact, rather than the ephemeral actual event, which makes a difference to us now; and the historical fact makes a difference only because it is, and so far as it is, in human minds."

(3) When is the historical fact? "It is now, a part of the present." Moreover, since they are in the same mind at the same time, images of past events are often, perhaps always, inseparable from images or ideas of the future.

These are the three questions Becker asked and the answers he suggested. From these ideas grew several implications which Becker then proceeded to deal with briefly.

First, the nature of historical facts means that no historian can present any event in its entirety. There can be no question of presenting all the facts and letting them speak for themselves. The notion is preposterous. In the first place he cannot present *all* the facts. In the second place, if he did they wouldn't say anything. He must choose a few from among many and in so doing he will inevitably "impose a meaning" upon them.

This necessity in turn implies that "the historian can not eliminate the personal equation." No one can completely, not even the natural scientist, but he can make a much better go at it than the historian because he deals with the external world and he can repeat over and over again the event he wishes to describe. "The historian has to judge the significance of the series of events from the one single performance, never to be repeated, and never, since the records are incomplete and imperfect, capable of being fully known or fully affirmed." And so "the same series of vanished events is differently imagined" by different persons and still more differently by different generations.

Our imagined picture of the actual event is always determined by two things: (1) by the actual event itself in so far as we can know something about it; and (2) by our own present purposes, desires, prepossessions, and prejudices, all of which enter into the process of knowing it. The actual event contributes something to the imagined picture; but the mind that holds the imagined picture always contributes something too.

A third implication Becker points out is that "no one can profit by historical research, or not much, unless he does some himself." Everyone may benefit from the physicists' discoveries about electricity, for example, whether he knows anything about them or not, "but with history it is different."

However, a fourth implication of the view that history

Carl Becker

is an imaginative re-creation in the mind is that every normal person knows some history. When he wakes up in the morning, his memory "reaches out into the past and gathers together those images of past events" which remind him who he is, where he is, and what he has to do. "History in the formal sense . . . is only an extension of memory . . . an enrichment of our experience by bringing into our minds memories of the experience of the community, the nation, the race."

Its chief value for the individual, is doubtless that it enables a man to orient himself in a larger world than the merely personal, has the effect of placing the petty and intolerable present in a longer perspective, thus enabling him to judge the acts and thought of men, his own included, on the basis of an experience less immediate and restricted.

A fifth implication follows logically—the kind of history that makes the most difference in the world is the history that the great mass of people carry around in their heads. Everyman's "ideas about politics and society," and consequently his actions, are partly determined by his picture of the past. It may be a faulty picture. The professional historian may have a much better image of the past, but he will never get "his own chastened and corrected image of the past into common minds if no one reads his books." This has in fact been the situation during the century from 1814 to 1914, when "an unprecedented and incredible amount of historical research was carried on"; in fact "never before has there been at the disposal of society so much reliable knowledge of human experience."

And what effect upon human life has this had? None,

or next to none, Becker concludes. It did nothing to prevent the World War of 1914–1918: "Governments and peoples rushed into this war with undiminished stupidity, with unabated fanaticism, with unimpaired capacity for deceiving themselves and others." If this was not the *fault* of historians, at least they did nothing to prevent it. They cannot complacently assume that it is not their fault if no one reads their books. The paper ends with an ironic comparison between the great influence natural science has had upon society (for instance in determining the nature of the war) and the negligible influence of history.

If there is anything revolutionary here, it lies in Becker's answer to this question—"What is the historical fact?", in the relation he describes between the historical fact and the vanished event: the fact is not the event, but an affirmation about the event. It is a symbol which enables us to "re-create" the event in our imagination. Once the historical "fact" is admitted to be not "something that has really occurred" (as the dictionary defines it) but a "symbol," "something that stands for, represents, or denotes something else (not by exact resemblance, but by vague suggestion . . .)," one can hardly avoid the rest:

Of a symbol it is hardly worthwhile to say that it is cold or hard. It is dangerous to say even that it is true or false. The safest thing to say about a symbol is that it is more or less appropriate.

This does indeed sound revolutionary and dangerous. The historian need not ask if his facts are true, only if they are appropriate. Appropriate to what? To his needs and wishes, presumably. What remained then to keep historians from being on the same footing with propagandists and advertising men? Well, nothing so far as that statement, taken out of context, shows; but this is one of the statements Becker deliberately formulated in provocative terms. In his files there is a note expressing this idea in preliminary form, and it indicates that Becker could not get away from a basic assumption that there could be some kind of real correspondence between an event and an affirmation about it. Even when he was in the process of reasoning out the idea that historical facts were really only symbols representing events, he circled back at the end to this basic assumption:

The historian is concerned with real events. e.g. Lincoln's assassination. But he can't deal with that event directly. . . . The historian deals with affirmations about it. . . . Very good he has an affirmation: "Lincoln was assassinated in Ford's Theater, April 14, 1865." Is the affirmation true? Yes, it is as far as it goes. Except that the *act* was not completed until death next day. But it is not the whole truth of the event. Another historian affirms: "Lincoln, sitting in a box watching a play in Ford's theater, in Washington, April 14, 1865, was shot by J. W. Booth, an actor, who then jumped to the stage, breaking his leg."—Is this true? Yes, as far as it goes. It includes more than the former. Well, any number of affirmations can be made, each true as far as it goes, but none being the whole truth. And no number of affirmations could include the whole of the actual event, simple as it is, because the event included every act, word, and thought of all those connected with it. The point is that the affirmation is a symbol which *represents* the event, and of this symbol we say, not so much that it is true or false, but that it is more or less appropriate. Appropriate to what? (1) to the truth of the event: (2) to the purpose of the author.[31]

Becker did not raise the question "appropriate to what?" in his Rochester talk because, perhaps, he realized that he would be contradicting himself to speak of *the truth* of the event as if it were knowable, but also, no doubt, because he knew that word "appropriate" standing unexplained would raise questions and stimulate thought. He smuggled the idea of correspondence between the symbol and the vanished event back in under his "second implication" anyway.[32]

In "What Is the Historical Fact?" Becker carried to a logical extreme his belief that historical facts were psychic phenomena, images in the mind of someone thinking about the past; he implied that any worries about their truth or falsity were in vain. He left the door open for such interpretations of his beliefs as that made by Harry Elmer Barnes, who said that Becker had shown that "the whole structure of 'erudite' history must be regarded as little more than a tedious and laborious fantasy, though it may be the best we can get." [33] If Becker did this, he did it by equating historical facts to affirmations, affirmations to symbols, and then by talking in such a way as to make easy the further steps from symbol to illusion, illusion to fantasy.

Five years after this talk, Becker gave his presidential address to the American Historical Association—"Everyman His Own Historian." Here Becker made an earnest effort to set forth his considered opinions, his real beliefs

[31] Notes, drawer 9.   [32] See above, p. 73.
[33] Harry E. Barnes, *History of Historical Writing* (Norman, Okla.: University of Oklahoma Press, 1937), p. 268.

about the historical enterprise. In so doing he expressed considerable preference for facts that correspond with what actually happened, and states flatly that the historian is "under bond" to be honest as he can. Philosophically "What Are the Historical Facts?" is neater. The lines of argument are sharper; the conclusions can be more succinctly stated. It was much more fit for a manifesto of the relativist revolution in history than "Everyman." But Becker was not taken in by his own logic and he had no intention that anyone else should be. He was keenly aware of the limitations of logical speculation, and, though he greatly enjoyed the process,[34] he did not feel bound to live by his conclusions when they violated some deeper demand of morality or common sense. Logically he concluded that historical facts were "in the mind." Logic could not define for him any kind of connection between those facts and the past events outside the mind; still, practically, he had to believe that there is a connection, vague, tenuous, and unreliable as it is.

"Everyman His Own Historian" is a much richer, more complex expression of ideas which were a great deal more complex than Becker's 1926 talk indicated. Becker himself continued to think "Everyman" the best thing he had ever written on the subject of history; [35] it is his real testament of faith in the worth of historical writing. It was ironic that his most positive statement should be taken as an expression of futility and despair by those enjoying more robust hopes.[36]

[34] For example, he scribbled out notes of various solutions of Zeno's paradoxes.

[35] Becker to Carl Van Doren, March 9, 1934.

[36] Dodd to Becker, Jan. 29, 1932.

His Conclusions about History

Becker gave his presidential address to the meeting of the American Historical Association in Minneapolis on a bitter December evening in the bleak year of 1931. All the ideas and many of the illustrations from "What are historical facts?" appear in it, but the emphasis is different.

"Everyman" loses much more by being paraphrased than the earlier paper does, but like all of Becker's writings it can be readily outlined. Becker proposes to get at the essential nature of history by reducing it to its lowest terms. First, he makes clear that he is using history in the sense of knowledge of history—he does not mean by history the actual series of events that once occurred; he means "the ideal series that we affirm and hold in memory." Then in its simplest definition "History is the memory of things said and done." [37]

It is obvious then that every person, Mr. Everyman, knows some history, although he may think he knows none. Mr. Everyman has to remember a great many things that have been said and done in order to carry on his daily affairs. Sometimes he finds that unaided memory is not quite enough even to keep his household accounts straight. He has learned to extend his memory artificially by keeping a memorandum book to which he often has recourse. But sometimes the memorandum book is inaccurate. It sends him to Smith's to pay his coal bill when it was Brown who actually filled his order. His note, "Pay Smith's coal bill," has conjured up for him a picture of a series of events that differs essentially

[37] "Everyman His Own Historian," *Everyman*, pp. 233–235. This article was first published in the *American Historical Review*, XXXVII (Jan., 1932).

from the actual series of events that occurred some months ago. Further research is required in the records —in Smith's and Brown's account books and finally among his own bills—before Mr. Everyman can correct his memory, satisfy his mind and pay his coal bill. This is history functioning in its lowest terms, but "functioning fruitfully and naturally."

Mr. Everyman knows more history than that, however. He does not live entirely in a practical world of coal bills and daily routine. He lives also in a wider world of memory and anticipation. He remembers his youth and the people he has known. Beyond his own experience he has artificial memories of many more things said and done by people he has not known but has only read or heard about. He carries jumbled about in his mind some sort of history of his country and, even more dimly, some sort of history of mankind. This remembered past will be only partly true, but it will be more or less useful to him—useful because it is somehow relevant to "his idea of himself and of what he is doing in the world and what he hopes to do."

"What then of us, historians by profession? What have we to do with Mr. Everyman, or he with us?" asks Becker. More than we may think. We, like him, do our research and create our picture of the past for a purpose. Our business is to be concerned with that "far-flung pattern of artificial memories that encloses and completes the central pattern of individual experience."

We are Mr. Everybody's historian as well as our own, since our histories serve the double purpose which written histories have always served, of keeping alive the recollection of memorable men and events. We are thus of that ancient and honorable company of wise men of the tribe, of bards and story-tellers and minstrels, of soothsayers and priests, to whom in successive ages has been entrusted the keeping of the useful myths. Let not the harmless, necessary word "myth" put us out of countenance. In the history of history a myth is a once valid but now discarded version of the human story, as our now valid version will in due course be relegated to the category of discarded myths. With our predecessors, the bards and story-tellers and priests, we have therefore this in common: that it is our function, as it was theirs, not to create, but to preserve and perpetuate the social tradition; to harmonize, as well as ignorance and prejudice permit, the actual and the remembered series of events: to enlarge and enrich the specious present common to us all to the end that "society" (the tribe, the nation, or all mankind) may judge of what it is doing in the light of what it has done and what it hopes to do.

History, understood in this way, is an ancient art, "still in essence what it has always been." It is a story of the life of man, a story with shape and meaning. Although now "the historian recognizes that his first duty is to be sure of his facts, let their meaning be what it may," he must also try to find and convey some meaning in human experience. He will not find it—no one will ever find it—by refusing to look for it, by refusing to commit himself lest the next generation say he found the wrong meaning. If he waits for the facts to speak for themselves, as the "scientific historians" have tried to do, he will wait forever. The facts never will speak for themselves; the historian, unconsciously if not knowingly, speaks through them.

In constructing this substance-form of vanished events, the historian, like Mr. Everyman, like the bards and story-tellers of an earlier time, will be conditioned by the specious present in which alone he can be aware of his world. Being neither omniscient nor omnipresent, the historian is not the same person always and everywhere; and for him, as for Mr. Everyman, the form and significance of remembered events, like the extension and velocity of physical objects, will vary with the time and place of the observer.

This is why each generation views the past differently, why the "new history" keeps on appearing. No matter how objective, how detached we try to be, we cannot escape our world. Historians must share in the effort of society "to understand what it is doing in the light of what it has done and what it hopes to do." Let us not forget our proper office, Becker is saying in effect; let us stop writing for each other—"history that lies inert in unread books"; let us work to correct and amplify the history that is living and working in the world—the history Mr. Everyman carries in his memory.

But we do not impose our version of the human story on Mr. Everyman; in the end it is rather Mr. Everyman who imposes his version on us—compelling us, in an age of political revolution, to see that history is past politics, in an age of social stress and conflict to search for the economic interpretation. . . . We are surely under bond to be as honest and as intelligent as human frailty permits; but the secret of our success in the long run is in conforming to the temper of Mr. Everyman, which we seem to guide only because we are so sure eventually, to follow it.

But of all this, Becker concluded, one thing only is certain: this view of history, like the work of the historian, is and must be temporary and will change "as mankind moves into the unknown future."

The reception of their president's address by the members of the American Historical Association was mixed. Of course the charm and grace of his style were expected and could be enjoyed by everyone, but many of his brethren disapproved of what he said, or were troubled that the speech made all their labors seem futile; a few were disappointed that it was not more revolutionary. On the other hand a great many American historians loved it. The relativist view of truth had taken possession of the minds of most of the young historians by 1931, whether they liked it or not; yet they still practiced with unflagging energy the rigorous critical methods of re-search which they had been taught. Becker's address rationalized this conflict to a certain extent: he paid his respects to critical methods of investigation, but insisted on the relative and temporary nature of the truths that would be attained, and above all, he showed the unique civilizing value of history, however tentative any one man's apprehension of the past may be.

Those who disapproved most heartily undoubtedly felt, as Theodore Clark Smith wrote later, that the Amer-ican Historical Association had been founded on the scientific principles of Ranke, that (history which inter-preted the past in terms of today's problems) was not worthy of the name, and that the relativist doctrines which had seeped into the Association and seemed about to engulf it ought to be resisted to the bitter end.[38]

Perhaps Becker erred in assuming that his address would not "make much of a hit with the general run of professional historians," [39] but he was closer to the mark than his enthusiastic colleague, Preserved Smith, who

[38] Theodore Clark Smith, "The Writing of History in America, from 1884 to 1934," *AHR*, XL (April, 1935), 439–449.
[39] Becker to Dodd, n.d. [Feb., 1932].

felt that Becker had simply disposed of the notion of scientific history for good.[40]

Becker frequently discovered that his taste for ironic humor caused him to be misunderstood. He was sometimes taken to be debunking men and ideas that he held in great respect because he wrote about them in his characteristic tone of gentle irony. Politicians have long since found out that humor is ambiguous and potentially unsafe, but Becker could seldom forbear to use an instrument which was so made to his hand and to his temper. Actually the joke he saw was the cosmic one; his irony was at the expense of mankind—the ridiculous and glorious animal, and it was mellowed and gentle because he saw the glory as well as the folly. He could never really agree with W. S. Gilbert that "man, however well behaved, at best is only a monkey shaved." His manner was ironic; his matter moral. Even his most appreciative readers, however, often thought he was poking fun at rather more specific targets. And so it was even with his presidential address to his colleagues, even with so old and close a friend as William E. Dodd. Becker's distress at this situation had the virtue of calling forth what he rarely gave—a long straightforward explanation of what he had meant to say:

I am sending you a separate of my presidential address. I was told that you were inclined to regard it as advocating the futility of historical research under a thin guise of irony. But nothing could be farther from the truth. I was led to this address by the necessity, from long back, of finding some answer to the frequent question: "What is the good of history?" The answer was not always easy, all the more so since it must be obvious that much of what is called historical re-

[40] Preserved Smith to Becker, Jan. 15, 1932.

search is a dreary waste of meticulous determination of facts the importance of which is difficult to see. I could have much sympathy with the definition of research which I once heard: "If you take it out of one book, it's plagiarism: if you take it out of many books, it's research." In seeking for an answer to the question, I was impressed by the fact that history as story is an old business. All children love stories. All primitive peoples cherish stories of their past, of their heroes and great men. From earliest times all peoples have their histories, true or false. History as we practise it is an evolution of these early stories, a more expert and sophisticated treatment of the subject. On the other hand, sociology, economics, and the other so-called social sciences, are relatively late developments. I asked myself what is the reason for this? Why is history so old and so persistent an interest in the life of all peoples? It occurred to me that there must be some natural and instinctive basis for this universal and persistent preoccupation with history. It must, I thought, meet some self-grounded human need. What that universal need is I have tried to point out in all seriousness. It is simply the need of a conscious creature, who has memory and who can anticipate the future, to enlarge his present perceptions by remembering things that happened in the past. The individual does this constantly, primitive peoples do it more or less unconsciously, and without much attention to accuracy. Critical history is simply the instinctive and necessary exercise of memory, but of memory tested and fortified by reliable sources. The facts may be determined with accuracy; but the "interpretation" will always be shaped by the prejudices, biasses, needs, of the individual and these in turn will depend on the age in which he lives. Hence history has to be rewritten by each generation. Even if the facts are the same, the slant on the facts will be different. You would certainly be the last to deny this I should think. At all events, my address was intended to find a natural and necessary basis in the nature of the human

Carl Becker

animal for the study and writing of history, to prove that history is a fundamental and most important branch of knowledge; to show that Mr. Everyman has and will have his history, true or false, and that one function of the historian is to keep Mr. Everyman's history, as far as possible, in reasonable harmony with what actually happened.

Of course I don't object to any dissent which any one may feel to what I had to say, least of all do I object to any objections which you may have to make to it. But I don't want you to misunderstand what I was trying to do.[41]

Dodd was not to be convinced, whatever Becker's intention had been, that the total effect of the address was not discouraging to young scholars—leading them "to a certain feeling of futility." He added, "Personally, I am not greatly out of sympathy with that, although on the whole my work inclines a little bit in the opposite direction for the reason that I have not yet abandoned the feeling that a broad and deep knowledge of history spread over the total population would be effective, at least effective in improving somewhat the tone and behavior of articulate people." [42]

To this Becker answered: "The only circumstance which would make historical research and study futile would be the achievement of what is so commonly thought to be the aim of research—i.e. the attainment of final truth. . . . But my thesis—that nothing can ever be finally settled makes the effort to settle it ever necessary and useful." [43] Although Becker wrote several other essays on one facet or another of historiography, "Every-

[41] Becker to Dodd, Jan. 27, 1932.
[42] Dodd to Becker, Jan. 29, 1932.
[43] Becker to Dodd [Feb., 1932].

man" remains the fullest, most balanced statement of his considered judgment of the historical enterprise, reflecting both his theoretical skepticism and his practical scrupulousness.

Both his earlier and his later analyses of the nature of history expressed one of these two divergent views at the expense of the other. Most of his pre-1931 statements emphasized the fallibility of the historian and the absurdity of his pretensions to objectivity and certainty. Many of his remarks after 1931 exposed the equally dangerous fallacy of supposing "that because truth is in some sense relative, it cannot be distinguished from error." [44] The different emphasis of his early writings and his later ones does not indicate a change of mind on Becker's part; it reflects a changed situation. Becker was a critic, not a leader of a school. When scientific, absolutist conceptions of truth prevailed among historians, he punctured them quite thoroughly. When a crude form of relativism, indistinguishable from utter cynicism, became the fashion, Becker attacked it with the peculiar bitterness of the man who sees his own words used to achieve an end he abhors. His own philosophical position had not changed; but his position relative to popular beliefs had changed.

For all that, the contrast between a very early article —say "Detachment and the Writing of History"—and a very late one like "Some Generalities That Still Glitter" is startling. It is indeed the measure of the change in the world between 1910 and 1940. In 1910 progress seemed sure and one way to hasten it was to destroy the notion

[44] Becker, "Some Generalities That Still Glitter," *New Liberties for Old* (New Haven: Yale University Press, 1941), p. 148.

that truth was absolute, eternal, and changeless—that what was true and good once would always be so. By 1940 that time had arrived which Becker had foreseen, when it mattered very much that all men should care what happened; but it seemed that what men must care about to save themselves in 1940 was the very faith which Becker had unintentionally helped to undermine —faith in reason, in objective fact, in the honest pursuit of truth.

Becker wrote three essays on the study of history after 1932, as well as many articles on public affairs in which he dealt in passing with ideas germane to the problem of historical truth. The first of the essays was on historical evidence. The manuscript is untitled and has never been published, but Becker read it (the title announced was "Limitations of Testimony as a Method of Establishing Historical Facts") before a small Cornell faculty group called "The Circle" in November, 1937,[45] and again at Princeton, March 31, 1938.[46] Later he revised it and probably read it again in the early 1940's. In this brief paper Becker attempted to answer the question "How much evidence is required to establish the historical fact?" For purposes of the paper he assumed that "any event is a historical fact if all competently trained per-

[45] Minute book of the Circle, Cornell University. This was a very small audience indeed, but a discriminating one. The Circle is an informal, self-perpetuating group of less than twenty male faculty members from various departments of Cornell University. Becker was one of the original members of the group, which was organized in 1934 by George Sabine. One member reads a paper at each monthly meeting. Becker tried out a good many of his essays on the Circle and often felt that the discussion clarified his ideas considerably.

[46] Becker, Pocket diary.

sons who have examined the evidence are sure it did occur." The question then is what kind of evidence will convince competently trained persons that some event did occur? Historians almost never deal with concrete evidence, only with the evidence of witnesses. Bernheim's rule, which has guided generations of graduate students, says that a fact can be established by "the testimony of at least two independent witnesses not self-deceived."

Becker comments on each of the terms of this definition; indicates how the historian must quiz his witness to establish his honesty and competency, and then he comes to the main point of the essay: why does a historian sometimes decide an honest and competent witness is nevertheless self-deceived? The standard reasons— excitement, emotional involvement, defective memory— usually account for the self-deception of a witness, but aside from these things there is something else involved:

This something else is not in the event, or the witness, or his competence. It is in the historian himself. This something else is the historian's inability to believe that certain kinds of events are possible, however much otherwise reliable testimony is brought to support them. When the historian is confronted with testimony to the occurrence of a specific event, of a kind which he is profoundly convinced cannot possibly occur, he always says that the witnesses, whether two or two hundred, are self-deceived.

So it happens that the historian proceeds to accept the testimony of two ordinary witnesses, or one for that matter, as establishing dozens and hundreds of facts; then suddenly he pulls up short and refuses to accept the testimony of hundreds of witnesses to a miracle. This, Becker says, is what we expect him to do "and yet if we inquire

Carl Becker

into it we perceive that he is really abandoning his normal procedure, denying the very presuppositions that he ordinarily relies upon to validate his activities." The historian tells us that he has no preconceived ideas about what has happened, that he sets out with an open mind to discover what has happened by an examination of all the testimony he can find, but all the while he has, after all, a definite idea "if not as to what must have happened, at least as to what must not have happened."

The preconceived idea . . . is determined by the climate of opinion in which the historian lives. Living in this climate of opinion he has acquired unconsciously certain settled convictions as to the nature of man and the world, convictions which interpret human experience in such a way that it is easier for him to believe that any number of witnesses may be self-deceived than it is to believe that the particular event testified to has ever happened or can ever happen.

The rest of this brief essay illustrates this point and defines it more carefully. Although this paper was simply an elaboration of a point that Becker had stated clearly enough in his first essay in historiography, "Detachment and the Writing of History," it was fundamental to his conception of history and well worth elaborating.

Another of Becker's late articles on the nature of history was "What Is Historiography?" which appeared in the *American Historical Review* in October, 1938. This essay, which proposes a new way of approaching the history of history, will be treated in Chapter VI.

Becker wrote one other article directly on the question of relativism which must be summarized rather fully since only a very much revised and compressed version of it has been published. This final explicit statement of historical relativism by Carl Becker was in the form of a commentary on the book *The Problem of Historical Knowledge,* by Maurice Mandelbaum.[47] Becker presented the longer, unpublished version of his criticism of Mandelbaum before the Circle January 20, 1939. A summary of this version will be given first.

Mandelbaum set out in his book to refute historical relativism. Becker proceeds, very provocatively—as he said himself [48] —to refute the refutation. Mandelbaum wishes to show that, contrary to the belief of many modern philosophers and practicing historians, objective knowledge of the past is possible. He sets about his task by analyzing in some detail the writings of three "relativist" philosophers—Benedetto Croce, Wilhelm Dilthey, and Karl Mannheim. From their works he extracts three "presuppositions" of relativism which he claims are held both by these philosophers and by such "practicing historians" as Carl Becker and Charles Beard. Once these presuppositions are refuted the foundations of relativism are gone. The first of these presuppositions of relativism is presumably from the writings of the historians: "No historical account can be objectively true because every occurrence described by the historian is demonstrably richer in content than any account can be."

Although Mandelbaum rapidly disposes of this first presupposition as an obvious fallacy of identifying "knowledge we may be said to have of any object with knowledge of all of the characteristics of that object," Becker denies that any relativist he knows "would say that we cannot

[47] Maurice Mandelbaum, *The Problem of Historical Knowledge* (New York: Liveright, 1938).
[48] Becker to Sabine, Feb. 5, 1939.

know objectively some things about the Declaration of Independence, or John Jones, because we cannot know everything about it or him."

The catch is that the relativist believes that the historian's account of John Jones or of the Declaration of Independence is based only "partly on objectively known facts and partly on reasonable inference drawn from the facts," and he realizes that if he happened to know a different set of facts about an event, the reasonable inferences he would draw might be quite different. To answer this, "Mandelbaum has to insist that every historical account is 'a tissue of facts' and nothing else," that even the selection and order of facts is objective—but that is the problem he deals with in refuting the third presupposition.

The second presupposition Mandelbaum finds in the writings of the relativists is that "all knowledge is relative to the situation in which it arises." He attacks this presupposition first by saying that it leads to absolute skepticism, since it "involves an infinite regression, which makes knowledge impossible." If every statement is to be judged with reference to the conditions under which it was made, then every statement about the first statement must also be so judged, and so on. Becker answers sharply:

To my unphilosophic mind this line of argument appears to be a species of logic chopping of the same order as that which proves that the hare can never reach the tortoise. It is in any case a begging of the question. . . . The relativist maintains with certain arguments that knowledge or at least historical knowledge, is relative. To these arguments Mandelbaum counters by saying that if knowledge is relative then it isn't knowledge, which amounts to saying that if knowledge is relative then it isn't absolute, or, otherwise stated, that if knowledge is relative then we are forced to accept absolute scepticism.

Again, however, Becker finds Mandelbaum's statement of the relativist's presupposition faulty because he has failed to distinguish between fact and inference. "I do not estimate a statement of fact, nor do I think any relativist would do so, with reference to the conditions under which it was formed. I estimate a statement of fact . . . according to the evidence presented. . . . The evidence may very well be adequate to establish the fact with so great a degree of probability as to amount to practical certainty." And, after all, Mandelbaum does not maintain that relativists deny this (as he should to be consistent). He says "that the relativist admits that historical facts are objectively ascertainable" and so he himself shows that his second presupposition cannot be a presupposition of relativism. But the relativist does believe the historical account as a whole will depend on the time and place in which it is written. Once more the real issue is the validity —denied by Mandelbaum—of the relativist's distinction between fact and interpretation.

The third presupposition of relativism, Mandelbaum says, "resides in the view that every historical account is dependent upon historically conditioned valuation factors." He admits that personal value judgments move a man to write history in the first place, but he denies that values influence what the historian puts into his account, unless, of course, the man is a propagandist and not a historian at all. The relativist, on the other hand, insists that, however scrupulous the historian may be, "the historical account as a whole is inevitably permeated with the historian's value judgments"—even though "facts are objectively ascertainable." This is the heart of the matter —"the point to which Mandelbaum, wherever he begins, always comes in the end, no matter which of the pre-suppositions he is dealing with." He has now got "to make good his contention that a historical account is a 'tissue of facts' and nothing else."

The substance of Mandelbaum's refutation of relativism, as Becker sees it, is in this paragraph:

Every historical fact is given in some specific context in which it leads on to some other fact. . . . Thus when a historian makes a statement of fact it is not with an isolated fact, but with a fact in a given context, that he is concerned. And in that context the fact itself leads on to further facts without any intermediation or selection based upon the historian's at-titudes, class interests, or the like. If this were not the case . . . we should have to appeal to our knowledge of the his-torian himself or to some general cultural value to determine how one fact is related to another in his historical account. That we do not do this, but consider the concrete facts as them-selves possessing a definite meaning, significance, and order, testifies to the non-valuational character of that which binds the facts into a historical account.[49]

Although Mandelbaum has two further chapters on relevance and causality "the object of which is to prove that events, as they present themselves to our contempla-tion, provide their own relevant and causal arrangement which the historian merely observes and records but does not create," they do not, in Becker's opinion, add anything to the weight of his argument. Indeed they merely trip him up so that he has to use the very distinction (between the facts and interpretation) which he started out to re-

[49] Mandelbaum, *op. cit.*, pp. 200–201.

fute. When he attempts to explain why one historian records "a different relevant and causal arrangement than another," he really "concedes the essential point in the relativist position." He cannot help conceding it, says Becker, though he does not seem to know he has done so, because "it is impossible to maintain that any historical account is 'a tissue of fact' and nothing else." In order to make a "connected and meaningful narrative" the historian has to arrange the facts in a certain order and draw certain inferences "from the facts as given and also from his general experience."

> I maintain that there is . . . a clear distinction between facts and inferences from the facts. And my point is that while the facts are determined by the evidence contemporary with the event and may remain unchanged whatever historian uses them, the selection and ordering of the facts and the inferences drawn from them, will always owe something to the purposes, biases, beliefs—in short, to the *Weltanschauung* —of the historian.

Moreover, there is a further question "which Mandelbaum does not even ask" which weakens his argument still more: What is a fact and what makes a historian accept one as established? After all, historians are ordinary human beings; "their capacity to assent to evidence, and therefore to accept an alleged event as a fact, varies greatly according to the individual historian, and still more according to the time and place in which they live."

Who then are the historians, living in what time, and in what place, who are to determine the absolute objective truth of alleged historical events? Who are the historians that are to guarantee the facts that shall be valid for all time? I venture to say that there are no such omniscient creatures. I venture to say that our knowledge of historical facts, as well as the inferences drawn from the facts, is relative and not absolute. The most that can be said is that the evidence for the occurrence of some historical events, and for an increasing number, is such that virtually all historians will accept them as facts beyond question: the probability of their having occurred is such as to amount to a practical certainty. If this leads to absolute scepticism, then all I can say is that absolute scepticism is what it leads to: I refuse to be frightened by any horrendous words that Professor Mandelbaum may think fit to discharge into the void.

At the end of his book, Mandelbaum lists seven reasons why historical accounts are from time to time radically revised. Becker picked out the third one:

Men have at various times singled out of the historical process events which were either totally disregarded by previous historians or were never consistently explored. Karl Marx's inauguration of a new type of economic history serves as an example of this. . . . Such new approaches to the historical process explain a large portion of the revisions which historical knowledge must always undergo. . . . Yet even in those cases where they demand an almost wholesale revision of previously accepted views, they cannot be interpreted as overthrowing the historian's ideal of objective knowledge. For it will be seen that they are accepted only because it is held that they are true; previous accounts are then rejected because they failed to uncover those historical factors which the new approach is in a position to recognize. The only conclusion which we can draw from this situation is the sorrowful one which is forced upon us in every field of knowledge: that no single generation has ever fathomed perfect truth.[50]

[50] *Ibid.*, pp. 299–300.

Becker concludes his paper by saying, "This I consider a very good statement of the relativist position, and in making it Mandelbaum effectively refutes his own refutation of relativism."

These statements from Becker's manuscript commentary on *The Problem of Historical Knowledge* differ considerably in tone, but not, I think, in practical meaning, from his expression of his beliefs about history in his published review of the book. There he said:

Since Professor Mandelbaum classes me with the relativists, I may be permitted to say that, so far as I am concerned, he has conceded the essential contention of relativism. I mean by relativism no more than that old views are always being displaced by new views, that the facts which historians include or omit, the interconnections between the facts given which they stress, depend in no small part upon the social situation in which he finds himself—in short, upon the preconceptions and value judgments, the *Weltanschauung*, of the age in which he lives. If relativism means more than this— if it means that a considerable body of knowledge, an increasing body of knowledge, is not objectively ascertainable, if it means a denial of Mandelbaum's statement that "the *ideal* of objective historical knowledge is possible of at least *partial* attainment—then I am not a relativist.[51]

A number of interesting differences are noticeable in the most cursory comparison between the manuscript "Commentary" and the published book review. The least important of these is the most obvious—the flippant, sardonic tone of the commentary is completely absent from the review. Becker would never have published a review

[51] "Review of *The Problem of Historical Knowledge*," *Philosophical Review*, XLIX (May, 1940), 363.

that ridiculed another scholar—particularly a young man publishing his first book—however strongly he disagreed with him. But more than kindliness operated to make him revise his paper greatly before publishing it. For one thing, he came to understand more clearly what Mandelbaum was trying to say when the members of the Circle discussed the question after he read his paper,[52] so he had more respect for the ideas, as well as a decent respect for the author's feelings, to restrain him. Moreover, looking only at Becker's definitions of relativism as he understood it, the "Commentary" needed revision for two reasons: (1) His statements of his own beliefs were not entirely consistent. (2) Consistent or no, Becker no longer cared to publish any statement of out-and-out philosophical skepticism, since he was appalled by the results of widespread epistemological and moral skepticism, half understood, and used only to destroy man's noblest aspirations.

Both of these points are satisfied by the book review as it appeared in the *Philosophical Review*. In respect to the first, both of the statements that seem to be inconsistent (if not verbally, at least in meaning) were omitted from the review, whether on this account or not I cannot tell, but one of the Circle members might well have said: "See here, you accuse Mandelbaum of confusion, but aren't you also confusing your practical certitudes with theoretical certainties? You say, in answer to Mandelbaum's second presupposition, that you do not estimate a statement of fact with reference to the conditions under which it was formed. You estimate a statement of fact according to the evidence presented. But you point out near the end of the paper that, after all, a historian's

[52] Becker to Sabine, Feb. 5, 1939.

inclination to accept an alleged event as a fact, in other words his judgment of evidence, depends greatly on the particular historian and the age in which he lives. What constituted overwhelming evidence to Joseph de Maistre that a miracle had occurred, carried no conviction to David Hume. How then can you help estimating the facts recorded by an earlier historian without some reference to the historian's beliefs and to the age in which he lived, since this tells you in advance something about the kinds of events he might accept as facts?

"It is true that you accept many facts as *practically* certain; you go ahead and use them; you do not seriously think they can be questioned. But then you don't think that they are really, theoretically, certain either. It seems to me that Mandelbaum's second presupposition is one that you *do* hold, *in theory*. You do think, after all, that all knowledge (including 'facts') is in the final analysis relative to the situation in which it arises. You say so in the end yourself—so after all you do not estimate a statement of fact simply on the evidence given."

In the published review, Becker avoided this hypothetical objection by omitting both the statement that he estimated questions of fact by the evidence presented, and his later statement that the facts as well as the interpretations were relative. He contented himself with showing that Mandelbaum threw away his own case by allowing that relativists do admit facts to be objectively ascertainable. And he indicated his own opinion about the slippery nature of facts in the following paragraph:

If we analyze what is ordinarily called a historical fact (John Jones was a certified accountant) we find of course that it rests upon other "facts" and upon "inferences" from these facts; and these other facts rest upon still other facts and upon inferences: and if we analyze an "inference" (John Jones, being a certified accountant, could not under normal circumstances have made the errors in the audit which he did in fact make) we find that it too rests upon certain facts and upon inferences from these facts. If we could carry the analysis far enough, the distinction between fact and inference would no doubt disappear. If we had all the data of all events, and a mind capable of grasping the data in their actual relations, everything would be immediately understood and immediately pardoned. In this timeless existence, there would be no occasion for "views," no occasion for distinctions between facts and non-facts, facts and interpretations, meaning and non-meaning, good and bad, being and becoming: everything would simply be, the entire blest *wie es eigentlich gewesen sei* would just be there. . . .[53]

As for the second reason for revising his commentary, Becker left his ultimate skepticism to be read between the lines by those who could do it, but he emphasized the beliefs which he held with practical certainty—the ideas which for practical purposes, he chose to act upon: a large and increasing body of historical knowledge is objectively ascertainable; the ideal of objective historical knowledge is "partly" attainable; and so truth is ever to be searched for, and ever worth the search.

This is the last direct answer Becker gave to the question "What is history?" The next chapter will be an attempt to compare those answers that Becker made at different times in his life, and to see what kind of a relativist Becker was.

[53] *Philosophical Review*, XLIX, 363–364.

III

The Nature of Becker's Relativism

For if reason is a functional instrument, then it must have a function, and what function can it have if it be not to discriminate the relatively true from the relatively false, the dependable fact from the deceptive illusion, in order that the organism may pursue the better rather than the less good interest? [1]

GEORGE ORWELL's novel, *Nineteen Eighty-Four*, has a peculiar interest to those involved in the historical enterprise because its leading character, Winston Smith, is deeply concerned with recalling the past. Since he lives under a totalitarian regime that enforces the exclusive right to play its own pack of tricks on the dead, his concern puts him into fatal conflict with the Party. Smith is the nearest thing to a historian that exists in Oceania in 1984. He works in the Ministry of Truth, helping to create the official version of the past, the only version available to anyone in Oceania. He does this by "rectifying errors" in the records. For example if a *Times* account in February quoted a leader of the Party predicting a rise in the food

[1] Becker, *New Liberties for Old*, p. 147.

rations, and in August the rations are cut, the earlier *Times* story is altered to show that the Party member made the correct prediction. The original record, which exists only in one copy in the Ministry of Truth, is destroyed:

Day by day and almost minute by minute the past was brought up to date. . . . Nor was any item of news, or any expression of opinion, which conflicted with the needs of the moment, ever allowed to remain on record. All history was a palimpsest, scraped clean and reinscribed exactly as often as was necessary. In no case would it have been possible, once the deed was done, to prove that any falsification had taken place.[2]

As Winston Smith sat at his desk under the watchful eye of the "telescreen," efficiently obliterating all traces of things said and done last year, last week, or yesterday, and replacing them with others, he began to want passionately to remember *the truth* about these events, and beyond that to discover for himself what really had happened in the more distant past, "before the revolution." His frustration and his sense of loss make him think a great deal about the philosophy of history embodied in "Ingsoc," the official philosophy of the Party. Many of his reflections on the theory of historical knowledge in 1984 have a discomforting familiarity, like this one: "The mutability of the past is the central tenet of Ingsoc. Past events . . . have no objective existence, but survive only in written records and in human memories. The past is whatever the records and the memories agree upon."[3]

"The mutability of the past . . ." Surely something like this is already a central tenet of most present day his-

[2] George Orwell, *Nineteen Eighty-Four* (New York: Harcourt, Brace, 1949), p. 41.

[3] *Ibid.*, p. 214.

Nature of His Relativism

torians. As early as 1913, William A. Dunning in his presidential address recommended to the American Historical Association that his colleagues "recognize frankly that whatever a given age or people believes to be true *is* true for that age and that people." [4] Many similar things have been said on similar occasions since that time. Becker's remark in the course of his essay "Mr. Wells and the New History" (1921) is one of the more vivid expressions of the same idea: "The past is a kind of screen upon which each generation projects its vision of the future. . . ." [5] This is mutability right enough—history is no more permanent than an image focused on a screen; the screen (which is the past) remains, but what we see on it depends on who is running the projector.

Even the most casual reader of the *American Historical Review* (or even of the *Atlantic* or the *Nation*) realizes that the scientific historian with his definitive picture of what really happened is an extinct breed; that the modest man who has taken his place does not hope to be objective, but only to recognize his own inevitable biases; that he does not claim to discover or to purvey *the* truth for all time, but only *a* truth for today, or at most, for this generation; that he is in short, a "relativist" of greater or lesser degree. He may not call himself one; he may prefer some softer-sounding term like "relationist" [6] but he will

[4] William A. Dunning, "Truth in History," *AHR,* XIX (Jan., 1914), 227.

[5] *Everyman,* p. 170.

[6] "Relativism is likely to imply indifference to enduring ethical and aesthetic standards. It carries a connotation of misjudgement due to personal idiosyncrasies and ephemeral pressures from which the judge has not made the proper effort to detach himself rather than a connotation of coloration due to cultural condition, 'climates

almost certainly be unwilling to accept the label "absolutist," unless he is a Roman Catholic cleric. Among secular historians, some degree of relativism can almost be taken for granted. Fifty years ago no such terminology was in general use, and it was not in use at all as applied to historians.

The relativist conception of reason and truth . . . was not invented by anyone. . . . It entered openly and above-board as an explicit presupposition of natural science, and from natural science slipped, imperceptibly, clandestinely, into the general complex of modern thought. . . .[7]

wrote Becker in 1936. But it had some help in the slipping after all. Becker himself was one of the first American historians to apply the relativist conception to history.

No one can doubt that Becker would have been repelled by Ingsoc in principle and in practice, as he was by totalitarianism in its less fully developed form in his lifetime. But no one who looks for them can long doubt either that he wrote many statements about history that sound strangely like the official idea of history in Oceania in 1984. For instance, does the description of history as "a palimpsest, scraped clean and reinscribed exactly as often as was necessary" conflict radically with its definition as "an unstable pattern of remembered things re-designed and newly colored to suit the convenience of those who make use of it"?[8] Is there any philosophical distinction to be drawn between historical relativism *as defined* by one of its most distinguished exponents, and the "muta-

---

of opinion,' and 'frames of reference' that no man can fully escape." (Louis Gottschalk, *Understanding History* [New York: Knopf, 1951], pp. 110–111.)

[7] *New Liberties for Old,* p. 33.   [8] *Everyman,* pp. 253–254.

bility of the past" as described by Orwell? Is Ingsoc's version of history simply a logical development of the relativist creed, a "final and fantastic form" of it perhaps, but still a form that violates no premise of relativism?

The answer to that, of course, depends upon what are taken to be the premises of relativism. If the three "presuppositions" cited by Maurice Mandelbaum and referred to above are accepted, the question might be answered one way; if a different set of premises is extracted from the writings of relativists, another answer could be found. What premises are found will depend on (1) who is doing the looking, (2) when he is doing it, and (3) where he is looking; or, in other words, what relativist he is reading. Or, almost equally pertinently, what work of what relativist? Or even (impertinently, *New Yorker* fashion) What page of "Everyman His Own Historian" d'ya read? It will make a difference, particularly if your analyzer and interpreter insists on thrusting a foundation of philosophical principle under every figure of speech that someone like Becker has sprinkled through his pages. Take sentences like these:

> The facts of history do not exist for any historian until he creates them.[9]

> We historians are thus of that ancient and honorable company of wise men of the tribe . . . to whom in successive ages has been entrusted the keeping of the useful myths.[10]

> The form and significance of remembered events, like the extension and velocity of physical objects, will vary with the time and place of the observer.[11]

[9] *Atlantic,* CVI, 528–529.   [10] *Everyman,* p. 247.
[11] *Ibid.,* p. 252.

Every generation, our own included, . . . must inevitably play on the dead whatever tricks it finds necessary for its own peace of mind.[12]

At first glance, these remarks would seem to serve nicely for the extraction of a set of presuppositions which actually fit Ingsoc, presuppositions like these:

1. The past is gone irrevocably; it does not exist for us.

2. Men, nevertheless, yearn to know the past.

3. The historian's job is to supply that need; to create and make known a past that will comfort and sustain us in our present endeavors.

4. Therefore, for the good of society, it is established that what happened in the past is what historians agree to describe as having happened.

Only one of the quotations, the third, does not quite jibe with those presuppositions. It implies that there is something of the past still around to be dealt with: "The form and significance of remembered events . . . will vary with the time and place of the observer." Remembered events are not very firm, but still they are something *given,* something to limit the historian. The past is not his to create out of whole cloth. To refer to the first definitions we compared, perhaps scraping a palimpsest clean and reinscribing it is not quite the same as redesigning and recoloring an "unstable pattern of remembered things." While Becker's figure is not entirely clear, it seems to suggest a mosaic in which the same pieces are shifted about into new patterns, rather than a parchment which is simply stripped and used for a second time. Once you begin to revise Becker's presumed premises along these lines, your eye begins to catch sentences like this: "Our proper func-

[12] *Ibid.,* p. 253.

tion is not to repeat the past but to make use of it, to correct and rationalize for common use Mr. Everyman's mythological adaptation of what actually happened." [13] And this:

Let us then admit that there are two histories: the actual series of events that once occurred; and the ideal series that we affirm and hold in memory. The first is absolute and unchanged—it was what it was whatever we do or say about it; the second is relative, always changing in response to the increase or refinement of knowledge.[14]

Obviously, the four presuppositions just given cannot have been Becker's. Equally obviously no self-consistent set of principles can be stated that will fit everything Becker wrote, every metaphor he ever employed about history. Nevertheless, Becker was substantially consistent in theory, and entirely consistent in practice, through forty years work during a period when a world of Victorian stability died violently and an age of intellectual and moral chaos came to birth. Any neat list of premises and conclusions purporting to be Becker's is suspect, and will surely falsify his ideas by their very systematization. He was not a logician; in fact, he looked upon logic as the antithesis to history. This is not to say, however, that his ideas violated logic. I do not think they do. His beliefs about history might, without great distortion be expressed in the following statements:

1. All men, primitive and civilized alike, want to know their past.

2. Certain things have been said and done in the past which have left traces in men's memories and in written records.

[13] *Ibid.*   [14] *Ibid.*, p. 234.

3. Some past events can be imaginatively re-created by interpreting those traces.

4. The extent to which the re-creation resembles the actual past event is something we cannot know, but it will depend upon (a) the quantity and quality of the records used, and (b) the quality of the imagination that does the re-creating.

5. Therefore, any re-creation of the past is only relatively true.

Or these beliefs might be expressed in the following way: All men need to know the story of their past in order to live satisfactorily in the present. Since the past events have vanished forever, no man can ever find out exactly what happened, no matter how long he searches the records or how patiently he waits for them to reveal their meaning. Therefore, the man who has taken on himself the job of describing the past can serve his fellow men only by using all his imagination, sensitiveness, and psychological insight to interpret and to fill in the gaps in the records for the purpose of telling a story of the past which has meaning and importance for his generation.

Obviously Becker's relativism has something in common with "Ingsoc," which holds that "past events have no objective existence, but survive only in written records and in human memories." They have the same first premise. But Ingsoc continues, "The past is whatever the records and the memories agree upon." Becker did not say that, he said the past was what it was; he might have said: "The past *so far as we know it* is whatever the records and the memories agree upon—only they rarely *do* agree. Say, rather, the past for us is whatever we can make out of the records and the memories." From here on the two doctrines curve sharply away from each other. The essence of totalitarian "relativism" is that the records and the memories *shall agree;* moreover, they shall agree upon whatever the state decides they shall agree upon. Orwell shows in *Nineteen Eighty-Four* how the technologically advanced state can control both the records and the memories to horrifying perfection. But this is only a pretence of relativism, used as an excuse for establishing whatever absolutism is convenient at the moment. This is relativism as some Marxists use it—as a weapon of offense only— to be thrown away the moment the old regime is overthrown and the communist system has established the final truth, the absolutely good society.[15] This is, in fact, not relativism at all; for it violates the primary assumption on which relativism is based. Becker on the other hand, was always aware of the assumption upon which he was operating, and was wryly determined to abide by it: "All philosophies based upon the universal relativity of things must be prepared, at the appropriate moment, to commit hara-kiri in deference to the ceaseless transformation which they postulate." [16]

I do not present this view of history as one that is stable and must prevail. Whatever validity it may claim, it is certain, on its own premises, to be supplanted; for its premises, imposed upon us by the climate of opinion in which we live and think, predispose us to regard all things, and all principles of things, as no more than "inconstant modes or fashions," as but the "concurrence, renewed from moment to moment, of forces parting sooner or later on their way." [17]

[15] Becker, *New Liberties for Old,* p. 36.
[16] Becker, review of Bury's *Idea of Progress, AHR,* XXXVIII (Jan., 1933), 306.
[17] Becker, *Everyman,* p. 254.

Carl Becker

From the beginning of his acceptance of the relativist view of truth, Becker saw this discouraging defect in it. In 1912 he wrote:

We never know what form progress will take until after the event. Opposing principles are reconciled by falling into chronological sequence, and socialism, for example, acquires virtue by the mere passing of liberalism into the limbo of yesterday. And this would seem to be the necessary result of a philosophy which identifies man and nature, thus reducing all values to the relative test. The price of not having dogmatic creeds is that the content of our faith is successively unfolded, as it were, only in the daily practice of it.[18]

Becker saw change as eternal; Ingsoc meant to "arrest progress and freeze history at a chosen moment."[19]

To our original question, "Is Ingsoc's philosophy of history simply the logical extreme of relativism?" the answer is no, so far as Becker's relativism goes. They both begin with the assumption that men can never find out exactly what happened. We cannot discover the absolute truth. Ingsoc concludes: we will choose whatever error we prefer, and establish it as official and absolute (taking care to destroy conflicting evidence). Becker concludes: since we can't ever know the absolute truth, we must be ever searching for the truer, and we must always be prepared to relinquish the truths we have in favor of others relatively truer.

Obviously the results of those two views of truth would be direct opposites. Under Ingsoc there could be no free search for truth. The truth did not exist until Big Brother

[18] Becker, review of Robinson, *The New History*, *Dial*, LIII (July 1, 1912), 21.
[19] Orwell, *op. cit.*, p. 154.

decided what it was. For Becker the most valuable possession of the human spirit was the freedom to seek the
truth. His fundamental assumption, more deeply held than
any belief about the nature of truth, was that "knowing
what is true is itself a primary value upon which all other
values must in the long run depend." [20]

This long comparison of Becker's historical relativism
with a fictional doctrine may seem capricious, but it has a
broader purpose than merely proving that Becker did not
lay down the foundation for history à la *1984*. I wish to
illustrate at the same time the crucial though apparently
slight differences between Becker's relativism and the
brand exemplified by Charles Beard. Becker and Beard
are usually mentioned in the same breath when the development of historical relativism is discussed; [21] their
names are coupled as enemies of "scientific history," as
practical reformers exploiting the past in the interest of
advance, as skeptics who abandoned an impossible attempt to be objective and deliberately chose a frame of
reference and wrote accordingly.[22] This is a misinterpre-

[20] Becker, "The Function of the Social Sciences," *Science and
Man,* ed. Ruth Nanda Anshen (New York: Harcourt, Brace,
1942), p. 243. Similar statements can be found in many of Becker's
later essays.

[21] Cf. Mandelbaum, *op. cit.,* pp. 17–19; Chester McArthur Destler, "Contemporary Historical Theory," *AHR,* LV (April, 1950),
503–529; Cushing Strout, "Historical Thought in America," *Virginia Quarterly Review,* XXVIII (Spring, 1952), 251–255; Barnes,
op. cit., passim.

[22] Not all critics of American historiography lump Beard and
Becker together. Samuel Eliot Morrison did not refer a single time
to Becker in his presidential address "Faith of a Historian" (*AHR,*
LVI [Jan., 1951], 261–275) although his object was to attack relativism. He took vigorous issue with Beard's theory and his practice.

tation of Becker, in spite of the list of quotations that can be cited to show their similarities. Becker certainly thought and said that objectivity was impossible, that all historians were biased to some extent; but he did not go on to suggest that they drop the ideal of objectivity and write with the avowed purpose of influencing the future in the direction desired. What he actually said was something like this: No man can discard all his beliefs, prejudices and interests and so make objective judgments *even about facts*. Some of his beliefs are an essential part of the mind with which he judges. Therefore let us not fool ourselves: let us not postpone making the best judgments we can until this impossible goal of objectivity has been reached. Let us write history that will be of use to the present generation, history which may influence what we do in the future because it helps us to understand what we have done in the past.

Becker described the difference between his own point of view and that of some other relativists very clearly in his essay "Mr. Wells and the New History." All historians, he wrote, must be interested in human "desires, purposes, and aspirations" and must "regard them as important in some sense or other. . . . But still there are different kinds of bias, different methods of 'exploiting the past,' different conceptions of the way in which its value for us can best be appropriated." First he described his own kind of bias (without saying it was his own):

We may be interested in the activity of man in the past as something in itself worthy to be studied for no other immediate purpose than the increase of human knowledge. From this point of view, the motives and interests that have produced wars and permitted politicians to flourish may be

contemptible, but it is important to know just how these motives and interests functioned, since they are part of the
record without which we cannot understand what kind of creature man is. The historian who takes this point of view will
perhaps say that whether Napoleon strikes us as a cockerel
strutting on a dunghill is beside the point, what is important
is to understand how, so recently as a century ago, such a
dunghill could exist on the earth, or such a cockerel so long
strut on it and with so much and so loud crowing lord it over
the barnyard. If we could once thoroughly understand this
cockerel and this dunghill, I imagine the historian to say,
perhaps we could understand our own cockerels and our own
dunghills, and so get rid of them. There is something to be
said for the view that we do little, in the long run, to get rid
of our dunghills by calling them nasty.

Then he described what he conceived to be the point of
view of H. G. Wells and of a good many American historians of the "New" variety:

But there is something to be said for the view that we do
little to get rid of [our dunghills] by indulging a mere idle
curiosity as to their chemical and bacteriological properties.
It may be, especially in times of pressure like the present, that
when a historian comes to a dunghill the best he can do is
just indignantly and emphatically to call it a dunghill, just to
make his readers intensely feel that so disgusting a thing must
never again be permitted to accumulate. From this point of
view, the historian is interested in the activity of man in the
past, nor primarily as something to be in itself intellectually
apprehended, but rather as something to be practically ap-
praised in the light of ends that are thought to be desirable
and attainable in the future.[23]

[23] *Everyman,* pp. 181–182.

Carl Becker

Obviously Becker had much sympathy with the historians who wrote primarily to influence the future in an immediate way. He thought they might quite possibly be more useful to society than the man who wrote simply to illuminate and bring alive the past, but he was not one of them. Not that he wrote merely for the sake of the past. Not at all. He assumed that knowing the past helped us to understand "what kind of a creature man is," and this we need to know "precisely for the sake of the present." [24] Still he wondered if the direct approach might not be superior in the long run, as well as more immediately effective. However that might be, he could not himself adopt it. He was not certain enough about the goals that were "desirable and attainable." Besides, after he had studied the records of ancient quarrels, and steeped himself in the writings of conflicting parties, he always understood too well, was too sympathetic with all the strugglers to be able to write with burning indignation or passionate conviction. He could not see that most of the wars and the pain in the world arose simply out of conflict between bad men and good men; he saw the more irreconcilable conflict of good men against good men. Thus he was deprived of the intellectual foundation one needs in order to write history which would be a weapon in the hands of the radicals. But it was probably "something deeper than conscious thought" that unfitted him for this role. It was a role completely alien to his temperament; in his own deprecating terms, he had "some kind of glandular deficiency" that made him unable to write the kind of indictments that Harry E. Barnes wrote in *The Genesis of the War*, or that Beard wrote in *President Roosevelt*

[24] American Sociological Society, *Publications*, VII, 93.

and the Coming of the War, 1941, or, for that matter, even in the less violent book, *The Idea of National Interest*. Becker's position between the orthodox historians and the New Historians was seldom understood, and it is easy to see why. He wrote devastating critiques of scientific history, critiques that did much to clear the way for the New History: he wrote generally sympathetic reviews of the books written by the New Historians. At the same time he pointed out (but not prominently until the late 1930's) the flaws in the New History, and he did not himself (except possibly during the two World Wars) write books that could be used as weapons in the hands of reformers or anyone else. As much as he might approve of Beard's attack on the sacrosanctity of the Constitution through *An Economic Interpretation of the Constitution,* Becker could not himself have written such a book. His *The Declaration of Independence* shows Becker's approach to another hallowed American document, and the contrast between the two books is sharp—not least in the fame and the sales records they achieved, as Becker would have been the first to point out. Although *The Declaration* is a delightful book and a well known one, it can hardly be said to have influenced the main current of American thought, as *An Economic Interpretation* did.

Becker's attitude was quite candidly expressed in a letter to Harry E. Barnes:

I received a request from the Editor of the Christian Century to write a series of articles [about the World War, 1914] in reply to yours. I wired that I could not reply to you because I was in *essential* agreement. I am, so far as the brute facts are concerned, and that means that it is no longer possible to lay upon Germany the responsibility for the war. Where I differ from you is in this: you are inclined to believe that some special persons are criminally responsible in somewhat the same sense that a man is criminally responsible when he commits a murder for personal advantage: and you are inclined, I take it, to think that by exposing the criminals the world can be enlightened & induced to take a radically different attitude towards war: I on the other hand can't see either of these things. It's a matter probably of temperament—some lack of vitality or glandular secretions on my part. You said yourself here that Poincaré et cie no doubt were, or thought of themselves as being, honest high-minded gentlemen who were doing their duty to their countries and therefore to the H. [human] Race—and if we were in their positions with their training and traditions we would doubtless have done as they did. That is exactly what I think:—"But for the grace of God, there go I." etc. Well, if that is the case, I don't quite see how they can be held responsible in the sense in which you hold them so. Another point is that "we the people" are perhaps quite as responsible. A people in peace is one thing: a people in war, or under conditions in which war is imminent, is quite another set of animals.

Well, this is why I couldn't write in the vigorous, superlative, sledgehammer way you do; but that doesn't mean that I protest, or that I don't enjoy what you write. I do. It can't, I think, do any harm. [This was 1926.] On the contrary it is probably the only way to jar people loose & make them think a little. You have done more probably to keep this question alive and make the people, or some of them realize that there are two sides to the question than anyone else. . . .

So I say, more power to your arm—and perhaps it would have more power if it were a bit more supple, & not quite so heavy.[25]

[25] Becker to Barnes, Feb. 21, 1926.

Nature of His Relativism

In short, Becker neither fought the reforming New Historians nor joined them—a position bound to be misunderstood.[26] He very rarely mentioned his private conviction:

The value of history is . . . not scientific but moral: by liberalizing the mind, by deepening the sympathies, by fortifying the will, it enables us to control, not society, but ourselves, —a much more important thing; it prepares us to live more humanely in the present and to meet rather than to foretell the future.[27]

This helps to explain how he could believe that history should above all be useful for the present, and at the same time why he was not a New Historian. This was his way of teaching *with* history, but he thought—his own philosophy required him to think—that there might be other equally valuable ways of apprehending history. Those who wished to use it to control society might be doing a different kind of good in their own way. So long as they aimed at humane and rational ends, he did not quarrel with them. Becker attacked extreme relativism and insisted on the pursuit of truth as the primary value only after he saw relativism in its "crudest and least defensible form . . . exalted to the level of a complete philosophy of life" and used to overthrow all faith in rational thinking, used to "identify law and morality with naked

[26] Cf. Herman Asubel, *Historians and Their Craft* (New York: Columbia University, 1950), p. 91ff. He says that Becker "tried to take advantage of the immediate usefulness of history" and indicates that Becker was more "present-minded" than Beard.

[27] "A New Philosophy of History," review of L. Cecil Jane, *The Interpretation of History, Dial*, LIX (Sept. 2, 1915), 148.

force as an instrument of will," used to make truth "relative to the purposes of any egocentric somnambulist who can succeed, by a ruthless projection of his personality, in creating the power to impose his unrestrained will upon the world." [28]

It should be noted that American historians who used the most extreme relativist conception of truth to discredit "scientific history" and who avowedly wrote in the interests of reform, were quite as appalled at some of the developments of the 1930's as Becker was. Harry E. Barnes, for example, complained bitterly at the young Marxist historians who wrote history according to the party line and who simply ridiculed the open-mindedness which distinguished the early workers in the vineyard—"men like Robinson and Becker." [29] The leading New Historians, Robinson and Beard, never in the world intended for historians to adopt a ready-made authoritarian definition of "advance" and write in its interest. They thought in terms of individual conviction, and conviction amenable to change when new evidence came in, but they did a lot to discount the virtues of the open mind; they helped to bring about the popular notion expressed in the smart saying "the completely open mind is one that should be closed for repairs." But then, so did Becker, even though philosophically he stayed on much more tenable ground than they did.

Beard's presidential address, "Written History as an Act of Faith," comes a great deal closer to Ingsoc than Becker ever did, even in Becker's disavowed "What Is the

[28] *New Liberties for Old,* pp. 144–145.
[29] Barnes, *op. cit.,* p. 394ff.

Historical Fact?" Beard had little more inclination than Marx to rest on a conception of truth which openly carries the seeds of its own destruction. The relativist, he saw, would be "executed by his own logic." In order to avoid this fate, Beard counseled the historian to confront "the absolute in his field: the totality of history as actuality." In order to bring this mass of raw material into order the historian must choose one of three possible conceptions of history: (1) history is chaos [this was a cowardly way out], (2) history goes in recurring cycles, or (3) mankind moves progressively upward. An ordering of events according to either the second or third idea of the past is possible "only by leaving contradictory evidence out of consideration." This he was prepared to do. This choice of a "frame of reference" is the historian's "act of faith" by which he can "help to make history," and so can avoid joining the "innumerable throng of those who might have been but were not." The ones who refuse to take a stand, who present history as meaningless chaos, presumably make up this throng. Beard chose to work within the third conception—to gamble on his prognosis. His frame of reference, "composed of things deemed necessary, things deemed possible, and things deemed desirable," pictured Americans moving upward to a collectivist democracy dedicated to isolationism.[30] This was not for Beard mere idle theory. *The Idea of National Interest, Open Door at Home,* and *American Foreign Policy in the Making* all show the theory in practice, though not so clearly as his last book, *President Roosevelt and the Coming of the War.* At the same time Beard had great respect for "scientific

[30] *AHR*, XXXIX (Jan., 1934), 219–231.

research," much more than Becker had. He had much less skepticism about the nature of facts,[31] poured a great deal more energy into accumulating them than Becker did, and had a great deal more faith in predictions based on them. Again, much of the difference between the two men stems, no doubt, from their different temperaments and constitutions. Beard was a warm-blooded man of action, Becker a philosopher who came near to agreeing with Santayana that "Historical research is . . . a servile science which may enter the Life of Reason to perform there some incidental service."[32]

Becker's relativism was not the sheer anti-intellectualism of Ingsoc or the New History of Robinson or Beard. Becker's relativism is a modest philosophy akin to Justice Holmes's conception of truth as "the system of my limitations." Becker too believed in certain things because he could not help believing in them, and these convictions about the universe, he thought, determined his conclusions not only about the values of life, but even about what he could accept as historical facts. "In this sense," he wrote in his unpublished article on historical evidence, "history is, as Charles Beard says, 'an act of faith.' But then no more so than all experience." If this meant he was a skeptic, then he was a skeptic.

---

[31] Cf. Charles Beard, *A Charter for the Social Sciences in the Schools* ("Report of the Commission on the Social Studies, American Historical Association," Part I; New York: Scribner's Sons, 1932), and Charles Beard, *The Nature of the Social Sciences in Relation to Objectives of Instruction* ("Report of the Commission on the Social Studies, American Historical Association," Part VII; New York: Scribner's Sons, 1934).

[32] Santayana, *The Life of Reason* (New York: Scribners, 1906), V, 52–53. Becker, Notes, drawer 2.

Nature of His Relativism

The position of the skeptic is not often satisfactory. Becker knew quite as well as any of his critics that skepticism must end in contradicting itself. If no knowledge is possible, then the knowledge that "no knowledge is possible" is impossible. If all truth is relative, then that statement itself is only relatively true, which makes it absurd. On the other hand, it was entirely impossible for Becker to believe that man could get absolute truth or any fragments of it. He could not escape the dominant thought of his own time. He saw the men of science "reconstructing the cosmos in terms of the evolutionary hypothesis"; he saw the pragmatists applying to truth itself "this law of change and adaptation which incessantly transforms everything." He came ineluctably "to regard the individual intelligence, not as an instrument suited to furnish an absolute test of objective truth, but rather as a tool pragmatically useful in enabling the individual to find his way about in a disordered world." Becker accepted logical pragmatism only in its milder form. He stood with those pragmatists who held that "the conception of the use, value, or consequences, of a reality form part of the conception of it"; with those who did *not* believe that "the conception of a reality consists solely in the conception of its use or value." Becker also never ceased to believe that "the conception of an object, situation, or truth . . . *is more than* a conception of its future, its results, its use, however truly the conception includes this awareness of practical consequences." [33] For Becker too, truth and error were still useful distinctions even though truth was relative. He thought that the truths men could attain were

[33] Mary W. Calkins, *Persistent Problems of Philosophy* (New York: Macmillan, 1907), pp. 559–560. Her italics.

relative to something besides their particular need or desire. That something was the unknowable reality, "the truth of the event," H. G. Wells's "God the invisible King," or, if you will, the absolute truth. There is no point in talking about "relative truth" if we do not assume some ultimate truth toward which we are trying to move, and Becker always did assume it. Moreover, he stated the assumption plainly in "Everyman," and in several of his late essays. *What* those absolute truths are he remained agnostic about, but *that* they are he had to assume. This was not merely a comforting fiction; it was a fruitful hypothesis. Without it human reason has no value; with it men have succeeded in "lifting themselves above the level of brute existence": [34]

Since prehistoric times the impulse to know what is true has been a human characteristic too universal and tenacious to be denied. . . . This tenacious search for truth and accumulation of knowledge has been the decisive fact in human history, the foundation of all the achievements that successive generations have commonly regarded as admirable, as having enduring value, and as therefore providing a valid standard for judging the advance or decline of human civilization.[35]

Even by the pragmatic test itself then, the belief that knowledge is possible, that truth exists to be searched for, is true. It has worked—to expand and to enrich the life of man. But by the same test, the belief that man can actually discover and seize upon ultimate truth, is untrue. It has produced only conflict, confusion and sterility. Those who think they have found the truth abandon the

[34] *New Liberties for Old,* p. 149.
[35] Becker, "Learning and the Life of Man," *Return to Freedom,* ed. Thomas H. Johnson (New York: Putnam's, 1944), p. 21.

search, apply all their zeal to propagating the one right way of life, and try to prevent others from searching further.[36]

This is the paradox Becker saw: one must take on faith something we can have no knowledge about—the possibility of knowledge itself. But from there on, one must be a skeptic, or the search for knowledge will be ended abruptly by someone's claim to have found it. If you would not have another man's absolute imposed on you, you must refrain from imposing yours on him; you must insist that you both may be wrong. If reason is to operate at all then it must have an object; this object cannot be supplied by reason. It is supplied by faith—by the conviction that truth exists. But if reason is to be free to operate, this conviction of truth must deny that its object is attainable, that final truth is knowable. Reason dwindles into rationalization the moment the answer it seeks is prescribed. The threat of prescription comes both from those who cynically deny that truth is anything but the will of the stronger, and from those who maintain that truth is sacred, imperishable, and changeless, and that *they have got it*.

Becker was distressed by the paradoxical nature of his conception of truth. He could not quite make himself happy by alternating reflection and action as Hume did. The Cornellian played billiards after a day of "philosophical melancholy and delirium" in much the way Hume had turned to backgammon, but the problem kept tugging at Becker's mind and infused a melancholy tinge into his writing. This is particularly noticeable in *Progress and Power, The Heavenly City,* and in the closing passages of "Everyman." Becker had a pessimistic turn of mind,

[36] *Ibid.,* pp. 12–14.

and the deplorable state of affairs in the 1930's depressed even the happiest of men, but the profoundest part of his gloom was occasioned by his failure to find any philosophical sanction for his private values. He wanted "to bring spiritual first aid to a harassed and perplexed generation" and he found it difficult.[37] If it was hard to get people "to go all out for reservations," [38] it was harder to show them why they should go all out for a paradox. Valuing reason and good thinking above all things, Becker was unhappy about having to believe that something other than reason determined the premises on which all his thought was based. When the war came in 1939 he saw unreasoned convictions, ancient loyalties and customs hold fast and "save the sum of things" against all the force of perverted reason. Only then did Becker come to prize these prior commitments as much as he had always respected them. Fortunately for us neither the cynical doctrines of Hitler nor the other-worldly, anti-patriotic idealism of certain intellectuals had really touched common men; they were still ready to fight for traditional beliefs which they had never analyzed and so did not realize were mere glittering generalities. Freed by clear and present danger to all he held most dear, Becker could at last proclaim with untroubled vigor his own convictions about the essential values of life. Then at last he ceased to agonize over the moral and epistemological contradictions men are involved in. If men had to perform an act of will by *choosing* to believe that truth exists before they could subordinate will to reason, then so be it. Men

[37] *Progress and Power,* pp. 12–13.
[38] *New Liberties for Old,* p. 126.

who practiced this inconsistency were vastly to be preferred to the monsters of consistency who denied everything but will. If, at the end, men have nothing to guide their actions but their preferences, at least they can prefer the values that civilized men have always believed good. Becker had always had this form of piety, and now he ceased to be embarrassed by it.

So far as his work was concerned, he had never needed to resolve the paradox of relativism. For him history writing was an art, as we shall further see; and he could practice it well and truly whatever theory of truth prevailed. His job was to convey truly his own sense of the past, his ideal history, to others. If it was to be worth conveying, his picture of the past must be formed by the play of imagination over innumerable facts and inferences supplied by investigation and tested by judgment and experience. To succeed in conveying the image in his mind, he had to do something a great deal less simple than stringing together pieces of evidence as they came to him. Flat presentation of facts which are literally true may convey to the reader anything but the truth, Becker noted:

"To render the situation complete, Caesar, though an avowed atheist, was at the same time Pontifex Maximus, and charged with the maintenance of all religious rites and ceremonies." This is a statement of fact. Is it true? The statement of fact is . . . charged with implications. The "facts" have an implication of badness. There is no objection, however, in a book of this sort, written for mature minds. It conveys the truth well enough for those who know enough of history & of Roman history to get what the author is trying to convey.

But suppose I put this in a text book for High School children. Would it convey the truth? Probably not.—at least not without more qualification than could be introduced.[39]

Three dimensional truth, in Elmer Davis' phrase,[40] requires something more than reporting "bare facts," supposing you can get hold of any bare facts. Three dimensional truth is not something that can be put down in black and white, something that can be positively attained, least of all by a historian. When the chemist describes what happens when a ten per cent solution of acid is applied to a bar of aluminum, he can just about tell all the truth he sees, but the historian can never do that. The more honest, the more sensitive he is, the harder time he will have.

Anyone who has written a text-book for high schools on modern European history from 1648 to 1927 in 749 pages, who has seriously tried to tell the truth of three centuries of history in that space, must have learned at least one thing: . . . that the truth of history, told within those limits, is not one but many.[41]

The historian can tell *the truth* only in the artistic sense of truth—conformity with his own conviction. The process of acquiring convictions should be hedged about with many precautions, but it should not be eliminated nor denied. When it is, it's all up with the historian.

Henry James, probably Becker's favorite novelist, maintained that the novelist and the historian search for the same kind of truth:

[39] Notes, drawer 2.

[40] Elmer Davis, "News and the Whole Truth," *Atlantic Monthly*, CXC (Aug., 1952), 32.

[41] Becker, Notes, drawer 2.

Nature of His Relativism

To represent and illustrate the past, the actions of men, is the task of either writer, and the only difference that I can see is, in proportion as he succeeds, to the honour of the novelist, consisting as it does in his having more difficulty in collecting his evidence, which is far from being purely literary.[42]

Becker was quite ready to bow to the superiority of art, but he thought the superior honor belonged to the novelist because he succeeded better in illuminating the important questions—not, surely, because he had a harder time getting his material. James little appreciated the historian's problem of making all his disorderly heap of evidence add up to believable characters or plausible incidents. Veracity is less convincing than verisimilitude. A good novelist composes three-dimensional characters who are somehow self-consistent, who fit the actions they are going to perform. The historian starts at the other end—with a mass of incidents—and has to work his way back until he can re-create characters who "strike the note of life," men whose actions seem to flow inevitably one from the other. "What is character but the determination of incident? What is incident but the illustration of character?" [43] asks James. If Becker could not accept this as an adequate philosophy of history, it suited the kind of history he liked best to write almost as well as it suited Henry James's novels. Both men excelled in portraying mental turmoil, psychological conflict, character confirmed by a minimum of overt action. The "synthesis" Becker strove for was not a compilation of "all the facts"; it was a unique production, as individual as a painting

[42] Henry James, "Art of Fiction," *Art of Fiction and Other Essays* (New York: Oxford, 1948), p. 6.
[43] *Ibid.*, p. 13.

by Picasso. For this reason he had little interest in the co-operative social histories that presented great masses of information without any unifying ideas. Although he was one of the editors of the "History of American Life Series," he wrote of it

I have never made any secret of my lack of enthusiasm for the kind of thing these books attempt to do. . . . All facts are "stubborn;" later in their fullness they become unmanageable: to make anything at all of them one must select and reject and emphasize them and subordinate and foreshorten.[44]

This was a job for one man to do according to his lights —not for a committee.

Becker poured every talent he had into writing history which might throw light on "the riddle of human existence." He tried to find out what kind of creature man is by examining with endless curiosity men who once had walked the earth, who had asked and answered questions, and who by chance had taken part in great events. He read their diaries and letters, their memoirs and public papers. He tried to see them as they saw themselves; he looked for "the unconscious influences that activate the human animal."[45] "The psychological question is the real one," he noted about the French Declaration of Rights. Emphasis on documents instead of on the thoughts and assumptions of the men writing them leads historians into absurdities. "One document can't produce another."[46] Nor can all your "method" produce a history.

"The cult of method," Becker thought, led sensible men to silly conclusions. It led Aulard to condemn Taine out of hand:

[44] Becker to Arthur Schlesinger, Feb. 14, 1933 (draft).
[45] Becker to Geoffrey Bruun, Dec. 6, 1931.   [46] Notes, box 2.

It is not Taine's conclusions that offend M. Aulard, but his method of reaching them. What M. Aulard can't endure about Taine is not the fact that he did not read the documents, but rather the fact that, professing to read them, he did not sit still in his chair and read them leisurely, methodically, without malice, and almost without interest—that is to say as M. Aulard has read them. I suspect that Taine found the documents so interesting that he often forgot to take notes, and so suffered the mischance of having more ideas in his head than could be found in his card cases. But alas! It is even possible that Taine did not use cards.[47]

Such detachment as Aulard required of the historian would in Becker's opinion, not insure fairness, but it would eliminate any chance of understanding. Sympathetic imagination was what was wanted if one meant to understand why men have behaved as they have. For this, all the insight and experience of life which the historian could bring to his task would not be enough. Some people would still defy comprehension. After reading quantities of papers of the eighteenth-century jurist, the Earl of Hardwicke, Becker confessed:

Hardwicke is impossible to get at. All these letters have not made him easier to understand. He wears always the mask, the armour of disinterestedness, & humility. Deprecates with solemn fun his "lack of ability"; assures us, with tears almost, of his loyalty to the King & the nation. etc. Is he a hypocrite? Reminds one of Uriah Heep, he is so humble. Not consciously a hypocrite. But one without sense of humor, who wears the

[47] Becker, "The Reviewing of Historical Books," *Annual Report of the American Historical Association,* 1912 (Washington, 1914), pp. 134–135.

conventional dress for ceremonial occasions & never takes it off.[48]

When Becker failed to get inside his subject's skin, when he could not put himself in the other man's place, he did not attempt to write much about him. But if, as he read, a person began to come alive, to take on familiar human shape, then Becker "listened with the third ear," [49] listened while unspoken desires and fears and secret inner visions were revealed, listened and thought and felt until he knew a character of flesh and blood. Then he wrote. Here in the execution Becker saw the whole value of history, as of all the arts.

[48] Notes, drawer 10.

[49] Theodore Reik, *Listening with the Third Ear: The Inner Experience of a Psychoanalyst* (New York: Farrar, Straus & Co., 1952).

IV

The Art of Writing

*If it be said that politics has nothing to do with literature,
or that the form of a document can be appreciated without
reference to its content, I do not agree. On the contrary, it is
a favorite notion of mine that in literary discourse form and
content are but two aspects of the same thing.*[1]

IF what Becker said about historical method was
unpalatable to many other historians, the way he said it
could arouse only admiration and envy. His philosophy of
history might be heresy, his research dangerously submerged, but his gift for writing was everywhere acknowl-
edged. In a period when historians were beginning to
condemn themselves roundly for ruining popular interest
in history by their bad writing, and were setting com-
mittees to study the problem,[2] a scholar who could also
write won rapid recognition. Becker's Wisconsin doctoral

[1] Becker, *The Declaration of Independence* (2d ed.; New York:
Knopf, 1942), p. xiii.
[2] For the report of the committee appointed by the American
Historical Association in 1920, see J. J. Jusserand and others, *The
Writing of History* (New York: Scribner's, 1926).

Carl Becker

dissertation was held up to students at Yale "as an illustration of what may be done." [3] When his first book, *The Beginnings of the American People,* appeared, Professor William E. Dodd wrote to Becker saying, "There is no one now writing history in this country who has written so well." [4] Soon that opinion came to be shared by others in the profession and out of it, as Becker's articles in periodicals like the *Atlantic Monthly* and the *Dial* made him known.[*]

The high literary art of Carl Becker was a source of wonder to his contemporaries as it is to later generations. To ask why a talent amounting to genius appears may be useless, but it is nevertheless interesting, and something may be learned about its development. Perhaps the excellence of his matter could be explained by his intelligence and scientific training, but where did the singular grace of his manner come from? How could a man who never ceased to look like an Iowa farmer write with the urbanity of a Lord Chesterfield, as well as with the pithiness of a Benjamin Franklin? The usual explanation for the polish of the "literary historians" of the nineteenth century will not do for Becker. He did not (like Prescott, Motley, and Parkman) come from a Boston family of wealth and cultivation where he was surrounded by books and literary conversation from his earliest years. Later in his life Becker was able to recall vividly the first time he dis-

[3] Max Farrand to Becker, Dec. 22, 1909.

[4] Dodd to Becker, Dec. 12, 1914. *The Beginnings* was published in 1915, but Dodd, as editor of the series of which it was a part, saw it earlier.

[*] This chapter was published separately by the *William and Mary Quarterly,* 3d ser., IX (July, 1952), and is reprinted with their permission.

covered reading for pleasure. He was eleven years old; he had never previously read a book or had a book read to him.[5]

Moreover he did not, like the "literary historians," enjoy a life of leisurely study in which he could pursue his literary interests without hindrance after his college days were over. Like most twentieth-century historians he had to earn his living by teaching. What was worse, he did all his teaching in small towns far from the stimulation many find in the variegated culture of a big city. His reputation as a sophisticated literary man, an epigrammatist, was made during the fourteen years he taught in that (to Easterners) most unlikely province of Kansas. Whatever it was that made his talent flourish, it was not the background and environment usually thought necessary for the development of humane letters.

What is it then that explains his "peculiar felicity of expression"? Can anything be said beyond what Becker said about Jefferson's writing and Sabine in turn said about Becker's: that it reflects "a nature exquisitely sensitive and a mind finely tempered"? Fortunately, among Becker's papers, there is some evidence about this tempering process, although unhappily it is scanty and cannot always be precisely dated.

First of all Becker had the fundamental requirement of a good writer—he wanted always and overwhelmingly to be a good writer. He had the urge to write, it was dominant over other desires, and it persisted throughout his whole life. It is an index of the enigmatic quality of his character that some who knew him very well indeed believed that he wrote as a result of outside pressures only,

[5] Becker, "The Art of Writing," MS.

that he did not have an inward urge to write. Professor Sabine in his fine and penetrating essay on Becker expressed this opinion strongly, and others have agreed with it. He writes:

Becker's historical curiosity apparently carried with it little desire to impart what he found; left to himself he would have been satisfied with the pleasures of the chase. As he said of Turner, "He was caught by his friends and set the task of writing." Fortunately, the charm of his style made him an object of pursuit by friends and publishers. Nearly everything that he published was occasioned by some demand other than the inward urge of the author. . . . The labor of writing was for Becker severe, and the facility of his finished work concealed much careful polishing by which that facility was finally achieved. Some kind of special inducement was necessary to make him write at all.[6]

Mr. Sabine substantiated his conclusion by showing that the genesis of most of Becker's books and articles lay in suggestions from friends or in the solicitations of publishers or editors of journals. This evidence can bear another interpretation, however, and another one is now demanded by the evidence of Becker's personal papers, which were not available when Mr. Sabine's essay was written.

Becker's own statements in an unpublished essay called

[6] George Sabine, "A Preface" to Carl Becker, *Freedom and Responsibility in the American Way of Life* (New York: Knopf, 1945), pp. ix-x. Apparently L. C. Petry and E. R. B. Willis, who read Mr. Sabine's essay, did not take issue with this judgment, and Geoffrey Bruun mentioned his belief that Mr. Becker's "impulsion to write was weak" (letter to the author, Oct. 19, 1950). Mr. Bruun added that if Becker wrote "on order," he seldom failed to transcend the limitations implied.

"The Art of Writing," and the less direct testimony of his journals and miscellaneous notes and manuscripts all indicate that whether special inducement was offered or not, Becker had to write. His own statement, written probably in 1941, is unequivocal: "The art of writing has been the most persistent and absorbing interest of my life." [7] And then, noting that the urge to write was something he "endured always as a malady rather than adopted as a racket," he says, "With the writers' malady I was infected at the early age of eleven. . . . From that moment my purpose in life was clear. I would be an author." To others who would write he continued:

If it be a question of writing really well, of attaining the something more than the correctly written, then it is first of all essential to have, in more or less acute form, what I have called the writer's malady. . . . For one who has this malady the desire to write will be, not necessarily an exclusive interest, but at least a dominant and persistent one. This is the first essential.

It is, of course, common for people to express an ardent desire to *be* writers who at the same time show little determination actually to write. If, however, a man says it has always been his heart's desire to be a writer, and if he has labored continuously to express himself well in writing, and if he has in fact produced books and articles superlatively well written (particularly when that required him to labor far beyond the demands of his assignment), then there seems to be no reason to doubt his diagnosis of his own case. Particularly is this true of Carl

[7] Becker, "The Art of Writing." Unless otherwise noted all Becker's remarks on writing which follow are from this manuscript.

Becker, who was as nearly without illusion about himself as about the world around him.

One further question remains: Did he write continuously, organizing whatever knowledge he had acquired, persistently trying to put in written form what he had to say (as he said a writer should do), or was he "satisfied with the chase," and disinclined to write except when pressed (as he evidently let most people think he was)?

Let us, with the question in mind, follow Becker's own discussion of how he learned to write and so take up the "second essential" before investigating whether or not he had the "third essential" in his list, that is, the habit of writing constantly.

"The second essential is the inveterate habit of reading, reading what is old as well as what is new, what is bad as well as what is good." The habit of reading is irresistible to most writers and usually precedes their desire to write. With Becker it was somewhat different. "A sample copy of *Saturday Night,* a weekly journal devoted exclusively to serials (then called 'continued stories') of the adventure, western, detective type" came into his hands when he was eleven years old. "At that time," he remembered, "I had never read a book or had a book read to me, or heard anyone talk about books or literature or the art of writing." But he was soon breathlessly involved in a story and at once a convert to reading for life. More than that, he found: "Quite apart from the story, there was something in the feel and smell of the cheap, soft, dampish paper—that had for me the essential glamor of romance." He made up his mind on the spot to "be an author, a writer of stories for Saturday Night."

This was the beginning of his career as a reader as

well as a writer, but the way was not smooth. His mother, unintimidated by modern psychology, was old-fashioned enough to ban *Saturday Night* because it was "not good reading"; he had to find other fare. He turned to the public library at Waterloo, Iowa, with "its immense collection of perhaps five hundred volumes" and began rapidly to make up for lost time—"ranging from Greek mythology to Eric the Red." [8] When he was about thirteen he read *Anna Karenina,* and Tolstoy came to replace the writers of *Saturday Night* as his literary model.

Although Becker's aim in life became ever more definite and clear, his reading before he reached the University of Wisconsin was not systematic nor did it give him any notion about how to proceed to become a writer. He set out seriously to seek directions to his goal during his freshman year at the University. He concentrated his full attention upon his rhetoric course, read Genung's *Rhetoric,*[9] his textbook, with great interest, and then, finding himself still without helpful instructions, "took from the library and read with equal care all the other Rhetorics to be found there." Though this was surely reading with system, it availed him little:

The Rhetorics did not help me much because to the unformulated question I asked them they gave no answer. What I really asked the Rhetorics was, "What must one do in order to learn to write well?" The Rhetorics all, without exception, replied: "Good writing must be clear, forceful, and elegant." I have sometimes wished that I might acquire great wealth

[8] This is Becker's memory of the occasion. His younger sister's recollection is somewhat different.

[9] John Franklin Genung, *The Practical Elements of Rhetoric* (Boston, 1887).

Carl Becker

and that the authors of all the old Rhetorics would come to me and ask, "What must we do in order to acquire great wealth?" I would reply: "Great wealth consists in a clear title to much money, forcibly secured in banks, and elegantly available for spending."

He came asking for a method and they gave him a definition. Although, at the time, he "took the definition for gospel truth," it budged him not an inch forward. In time he learned from experience what the rhetorics failed to teach him. Finding his way by himself, he decided that there are things that one can do in order to learn to write well and one of these is simply to read. What sort of reading? Wide and constant reading and only partly for information.

The writer will read for information, but also with an ear always open to catch the meaning and overtones of words and the peculiar pitch and cadence of their arrangement. There will thus be deposited in the mind, in the subconscious if you prefer, an adequate vocabulary, and a sure feeling for the idioms, rhythms, and grammatical forms that are natural to the language. In time these become so much a part of the writer's mentality that he thinks in terms of them, and writes properly by ear, so to speak, rather than by rule. Thinking too precisely on the rule is apt to give one's writing a certain correct rigidity, even a slightly archaic quality, often found in the writing of professors.

It would be hard to find a page in any of Becker's mature writing that does not prove the validity of this advice.

He developed gradually a complete mastery of the art of writing by ear. So literally was this true that he once told some of his students "that he had a feeling for how a sentence should sound even before he wrote it, and did not consider it complete until it sounded the way he thought it ought to have sounded." [10] When it did sound right that was how it stayed. He allowed no prejudice against split infinitives or against ending sentences with prepositions to distort his prose into ambiguous or stilted English. For example, a line in "Everyman His Own Historian" reads: "The exact truth of remembered events he has in any case no time, and no need, to curiously question or meticulously verify." [11] Altered to read: "Curiously to question or meticulously to verify," it sounds pedantic and sing-song. "To question curiously or verify meticulously," still sounds a little polysyllabic, and it is impossible because putting "curiously" after instead of before "question" in some mysterious way makes it ambiguous. "To question curiously" could mean "in a strange way" instead of "inquisitively," which is clearly what it means in "to curiously question." Moreover the very sound, the alliteration or the rhythm, of the words as they stand imparts a delicate irony to the sentence which would be lost in any recasting. After the time Becker must have spent on this sentence, after the nice discrimination he had exercised, it would have been no wonder if he had exploded when he discovered his assistant, as yet too young to be free of the tyranny of convention, attempting to "unsplit" his infinitive for him while proofreading the paper. There was no explosion, but the young man did not soon forget his chagrin, nor the fact that split in-

[10] Louis Gottschalk to George B. Gilkey, Feb. 4, 1949 (copy in Gottschalk files).
[11] Page 246.

finitives are not always used by accident or by the uninitiated.[12]

Another and a more surprising confirmation of the fact
that Becker really wrote by ear is that his spelling is shaky.
The repeated spelling in his handwritten manuscripts of
such a word as "mayhem" as "mahem," or "germane" as
"germain" is surely unusual for a constant reader. A more
obvious result of his concern with the sounds of words is
that his sentences (whether written for lectures or not)
seldom have any grating consonants or shaggy sibilants.
They want to be read aloud. When so read they slip
smoothly off the tongue and into the mind; there are no
rough edges, nothing strange and harsh in the rhythms or
in the words. The words are honest English of respectable
age or the native American of the man in the street, but
never synthetic jargon. The abrupt change of pace he
achieved by the juxtaposition of rather stately English
with the commonest speech gave character and vitality
to a passage like this one: "If logic presumes to protest in
the name of the law, they know how to square it, so that it
complaisantly looks the other way." [13] Although he knew
and used the findings of the newer social sciences, an-
thropology, sociology, and Freudian psychology, he for-
bore to use their special terms. What is more he learned to
avoid ugly compound words like "democratization" and
"historiography," awkward alliterations like "procedural

[12] Val Lorwin was Becker's assistant from 1931 to 1932. He
wrote in a letter to David Hawke, April 10, 1950: "I proofread
his [Becker's] AHA presidential address, and had the effrontery to
try to unsplit an infinitive in it. He had split it deliberately, and
he quietly put me in my place."

[13] *The Heavenly City of the Eighteenth Century Philosophers*
(New Haven: Yale University Press, 1932), p. 26.

postulates," and multisyllable words that are jolting and unrhythmical.

The language of Shakespeare and the King James Bible had been so early deposited in his mind and so completely assimilated that it became part of the very fabric of his prose: "Kansans love each other for the dangers they have passed." [14] "Let not the harmless, necessary word 'myth' put us out of countenance." [15] "I do not present this view of history as one that is stable and must prevail." [16] Often the cadence alone is directly reminiscent of some forgotten classic that can be recalled, but it may be too subtle for that. For example, "It is not possible, it is not essential . . ." [17] brings to mind at once "We cannot consecrate, we cannot hallow this ground. . . ." But another line "Not a life of drudgery, or genius itself shall avoid disaster," [18] is much harder to pin down, though just as haunting. Whether actually familiar in cadence or not, his sentences fall pleasantly on the ear; they are traditional and melodic, never strange and discordant. He kept to the old tonal system, but the tunes are seldom trite.

There is more than the evidence of his writing, though that is sufficient, to prove that Becker saturated himself in literature of all sorts. The twenty-drawer cabinet of research notes which are now in the Cornell University Library prove that he was not only a constant reader of catholic taste, but he was what is much rarer, a participative reader. His reading notes are not so much voluminous as thoughtful. He attended closely; he stayed oriented by any aids he found necessary—often drawing rather clumsy

[14] Becker, "Kansas," *Everyman,* p. 24.   [15] *Everyman,* p. 247.
[16] *Ibid.,* p. 254.   [17] *Ibid.,* p. 245.
[18] *Atlantic Monthly,* CVI, 525.

little maps or diagrams; he questioned and reflected upon the author's inferences; he pursued striking ideas out into his own realms of being. All these things he might do whether he was reading a study of the French Revolution, a philosophical essay, or a novel.

Although his reading was broad, it was discriminating and it was not superficial. His reading notes do not indicate that he tried to "read everything," but rather that he read all kinds of things. He was interested in almost all forms of human endeavor and in every type of human behavior. He read with care about them all. Two exceptions should be noted. Music and painting—perhaps the fine arts in general—meant little to Becker. Agreeing as he did with Pascal that "thought makes the dignity of man" he had little comprehension of activities in which emotions and not ideas are the molding force. After a visit to the Louvre he wrote: "The great mass of paintings do not interest me, because I know nothing. It is a language I do not understand. Like music, I don't know enough about what they were driving at, how they tried to get their effects, how far they succeeded and how far failed." [19] A few paintings—especially the "Mona Lisa"—and some of the sculpture—ancient Greek and Roman—did interest him. It was an intellectual, speculative interest in the people represented, however, not primarily an esthetic concern.

His interest in the thoughts of human beings was otherwise unlimited. Mathematical reasoning (if not too technical for him to follow) or even mystical revelations commanded his attention; indeed all the various ways

[19] European diary, Aug. 29, 1924.

men attempt to understand and come to terms with the universe, whether through science, religion, or simply daydreams, were of profound interest to him. He believed that great novels, poetry, and drama deal with the fundamental problems of the individual confronting the universe and are therefore a less ephemeral form of literature than history which deals with superficial affairs and temporary institutions.[20] It is not surprising, then, that Shakespeare and Henry James bulk almost as large as Santayana and Bertrand Russell among his miscellaneous notes, and these last two are probably quoted oftener and at greater length than any other modern writers. Bits from Plato's Dialogues stand next to notes on Browning's *The Ring and the Book* or others from T. S. Eliot or Anatole France. These are all notes in the handwriting of his mature years—not remains of his school days.

It is clear that Becker read more fiction than most scholars feel that they have time for. Probably his historical perception as well as his writing was the better for it. His psychological insight—one quality that lifts his biographical studies so far out of the general run—was based partly on the study of Freud and other psychologists, no doubt, but possibly more upon the knowledge of people gained through literature. He was with Santayana, a "literary psychologist." Madame Roland was more understandable in the light of Flaubert's picture of Madame Bovary. The clues are easier to pick up—indeed can only be picked up—if one has the experience to recognize them. Becker's close acquaintance through books with three dimensional people of all social and moral

[20] Notes, drawer 9.

conditions undoubtedly gave life and depth to his historical studies such as no knowledge of "case studies" or "economic man" could have given them.

Yet he did not ignore economic man or any aspect of man which could be discerned and commented upon. All that man had thought or done (including his thoughts about his own thinking) were history in Becker's definition and in his practice, so any clear distinction between his notes on history and those on literature or philosophy or "general reading" is impossible. Yet some classification is possible. Most of his notes are obviously directly related to courses he taught or books he wrote. They contain factual information, interpretation of events and so forth. But one significant part of the notes is of a more unusual description—a category he labeled "Form and Substance."

This group of notes shows that he did not give up finding direct help in learning to write after his disappointment with the rhetorics in his college days. In later years he read and carefully noted such hints as the masters of the craft let fall. Aristotle, Virginia Woolf, Marcel Proust, and Van Wyck Brooks appear among others, but Henry James and Remy de Gourmont seem to have carried more weight with him than any others, except perhaps Pascal whose ideas were peculiarly congenial to Becker. No single author influenced his style noticeably either by precept or example, but he was peculiarly indebted to one period. His aim and his achievement in writing were essentially those of the eighteenth century. "That is best wrote which is best adopted for obtaining the end of the writer," said Benjamin Franklin, and Becker found that definition satisfactory when he discarded the dogma of his nineteenth-century rhetoric books that "good writing must be clear, forceful, and elegant." He read more in and about the eighteenth century than any other; he found it congenial; and eighteenth-century writers must have influenced or at least confirmed his taste for clarity, precision and simplicity in prose.

Hints and standards of excellence were all very well, but Becker early divined that no royal road was to be found and set himself to follow the long and difficult path of self-corrective experience. First, experience through literature: "Abstain and buy books," he peremptorily reminded himself in his college journal! [21] Next, experience through writing.

The third and most important thing to be done in order to learn to write well is to write. Never let anyone persuade you to refrain from writing until you have something to say—something important is always meant. As well tell the child to refrain from talking until he has learned to speak correctly. It is only by incessant practice in the way of gurgles and noises that he learns to speak at all; and it is only by writing much sad stuff that anyone can learn to write something good enough even, as De Gourmont says, to merit a prize for literary excellence. Whether what one writes is important or not is another matter. That depends upon native intelligence and knowledge. But one thing is certain: there is no better way of developing whatever knowledge one may have acquired, than by persistently trying to put in written form what one has to say, whether important or not. Fortunately those who are infected with the writer's malady will pay no attention to this bad advice. They will write because they must, filling pages and pages, as well aware as any one that what they write isn't important, but always hoping that in time it

[21] "Wild Thoughts Notebook," undated entry [May, 1895].

may be, and at all events determined to say what they find to say, whether important or not, as well as they can.[22]

The question of whether Becker actually did develop his own talent according to these instructions seems to be answered in the affirmative by the papers now in the Cornell University Library. There is much to show that he was always writing as well as he could—and frequently (before he had mastered his craft) just for the practice or in response to an inner urge.

The earliest examples of his writing are the two pocket-sized notebooks which he kept from January, 1894, to May, 1895, during his second and third years at the University of Wisconsin—the "Wild Thoughts Notebooks." After the last dated entries in the second notebook he jotted down all sorts of odds and ends—quotations in English, French, German, and Italian, bits of poetry (some his own), and epigrammatic remarks that bear a close resemblance to his later writings. His characteristic habit of taking a cliché and twisting it in a surprising way is very much in evidence in these early scribblings. He was practicing an art of which he became a master: "A little conscience is a dangerous thing." "Some men are born stupid. And some achieve stupidity." "One man's lust is another's love." Pieces of advice which he was to cleave unto all the days of his life appear: " 'An author should consider how far the art of writing consists in knowing what to leave in the inkstand.' Lowell."

These "Wild Thoughts" are never diaries but the notebooks of an apprentice writer. One day he attempted to record a dialect conversation heard in the street (No-

[22] "Art of Writing."

vember 11, 1894). Another time he told a melancholy little tale of the unrequited love of a boy in his rooming house for a ballet dancer who stayed in Madison for a week (March 24, 1894). Several times he tried to describe the audience (and even himself watching the audience!) in the town opera house while he sat in the upper gallery waiting for a play to begin (February 5, 6, 1894). Again he wandered into the park and sat on an iron bench and waited until a man eager to talk about his grievances came along and gave him material for a character sketch with plenty of authentic dialogue (June 12, 1894). Frequently he outlined the life story of a real or imaginary person who had somehow come to a desperate pass; then he left it with a query about whom to blame—society or the individual (March 14, 17, 1894). Not only was he trying hard to say well what he had to say, but also he was trying to develop more important things to say by examining the behavior and motivation of all sorts of people, and by broadening and deepening his own experience. He reflected at length upon the advice of William Dean Howells which he copied into his notebook:

For this work [realistic fiction] the young writer needs expression and observation not so much of others as of himself, for ultimately his characters will all come out of himself and he will need to know motive and character with such thoroughness and accuracy as he can acquire *only* through his own heart [February 10, 1894].

The "Wild Thoughts Notebooks" throw an interesting light on the mind and thought of Carl Becker during his undergraduate days, but the clearest message in them is that he was then earnestly training himself to be a writer. Moreover the inference is unavoidable that he was already an observer far more than he was a participator in the life around him.

It was not writing history, to be sure, that he had in mind at that time. He wanted to write novels, "as good as *Anna Karenina*," as he recalled it almost fifty years later.[23] His old notes in their faded ink confirm that it was a deeply felt desire. That he kept some tenderness toward his youthful strivings may be inferred from the fact that he preserved all of his life these records of a day that was gone. Among the files he left to Cornell University, there are no other papers of any kind written during his undergraduate years, unless it be a few undated research notes.

Why Becker turned aside from the pursuit of his first ambition is not entirely clear. There was probably a slow curving of his path rather than an abrupt turn; in any case the new course was not so far from the old as to preclude his reaching the original goal eventually. In "The Art of Writing" Becker dropped the autobiographical thread after describing his first year at the university. The thread may be picked up just beyond that point in his earlier article on Frederick Jackson Turner. There he said that he was "infected with the desire to study history" during his junior year (1895) after prolonged exposure to Turner and to Charles Homer Haskins. It is significant, however, that this infection was only his old "writer's malady" in a new form. It was not, he admits, until he ceased to see Turner as a teacher and began to see him as " 'historian' . . . better still 'author' " that he "brought out [his] tiny little wagon and fumblingly hitched it to that bright particular star." [24]

[23] "Art of Writing."
[24] "Frederick Jackson Turner," *Everyman*, pp. 195–200.

Art of Writing

Although the "Wild Thoughts Notebook" of 1895 is the last evidence that Becker was consciously preparing to write fiction, there is much to show that he kept on practicing writing as an art, simply for its own sake, if no immediate purpose offered. He did so during at least one other period of his life by means of a journal. From June 15, 1924 to September, 1924, while making his only trip to Europe, he wrote to his fourteen-year-old son daily accounts of the things he saw and did. This journal served the double purpose of keeping his family informed and of making a record of his trip for himself, as well as giving him practice during a time when he was doing no historical writing. That the last was by no means the least reason for writing the 1924 diary is fairly clear from its contents. It abounds in detailed physical descriptions— of his cabin on shipboard, of Scottish landscapes and castles, of cathedrals in England and France, of Paris streets, of palaces and gardens and trains. It is all quite factual and admirably pitched to the level of interest and understanding of a fourteen-year-old. His descriptions of mechanical gadgets—like the ship's log-line, and the equipment in his cabin on the "S.S. Columbia" are really exercises in clarity and precision of expression. Whether he knew it at the time or not, Becker was laying up for himself experience for the difficult task of writing a textbook for high-school students. Wherever he discussed for his son the history of the places he described, he did it very simply yet without condescension, in the manner of his *Modern History*.

Perhaps more significant than his brief journals was his lifelong habit of making and filing away notes of his ideas and reflections upon books, people and events; these notes testify that he liked to express himself in writing. The kind of vagrant thought that most people would dissipate in conversation and have done with, he would ruminate upon until all its implications came to light and then he would write it out in full and file it away among his research notes. Many of these notes appeared later in clearer form in his published writings; many of them did not, in any recognizable way. A sample of one of his briefer notes is given here:

"To understand all is to pardon all." This expresses a truth but not exactly. "Understand" is a function of impersonal intelligence. "Pardon" is an expression of a moral judgment. The two have really little or nothing in common. When you understand all, you "pardon" all only in the sense that you understand that things must be as they are and not otherwise. If I knew all about, say a brutal gangster and kidnapper, I might well know that he was not "responsible," that he could not have been otherwise. Yet I might not "pardon" him; I might judge that he should be shot. Just as I would crush a rattlesnake. Then my "understanding" could also understand this, that I should still not pardon him but kill him.—And still I might not "pardon" myself for not "pardoning" the gangster who could not be otherwise: and my understanding would understand this also. To understand all is to understand —among the all, the refusal to pardon those who cannot do otherwise than they do [Drawer 2].

Notes of this type seem to bespeak a custom of thinking on paper, and so not thinking vaguely but with some form and direction.

Although almost all of Becker's finished work was published, there are more extended writings among his files that were evidently not written in response to any urging but that of his own nature. By the time he reached maturity he had enough to say and had learned how to say it so well, that he was almost never in want of a market. Nevertheless there was one period—a few years immediately after the First World War—when his literary fortunes were at a low ebb. Grave personal cares—his stepdaughter's incurable illness and the beginning of his own painful digestive ailment—must explain it to a large degree, but aside from that the war and even more its aftermath of "normalcy" were profoundly disturbing to him. It was not only his faith in democracy that was blighted by disgust; his faith in himself and in his work suffered as well.

His first postwar book, *The United States: An Experiment in Democracy,* reflects both. It was written at the request of his former colleague, Guy Stanton Ford, for use by the Creel Committee in its overseas information program, but by the time the manuscript was finished the war had ended.[25] The committee ceased all publication and Becker sought a private publisher. It was declined by Scribner's [26] before it was accepted by Harper's in 1920. *The United States* is the only book Becker ever wrote that seldom rises above being, for him, merely competently written. Its flatness is exaggerated by comparison with its immediate predecessor—the sparkling *Eve of the Revolution.* For its original purposes it might have been excellent [27]—it was to have been translated into many different languages and distributed as a sort of handbook

[25] Guy Stanton Ford to author, July 11, 1952.

[26] Scribner's to Becker, Oct. 17, 1919.

[27] Mr. Ford has found it the best one-volume history for foreigners (letter, July 11, 1952).

of American history and government—but it lacks the characteristic flavor and subtlety of Becker's other books. Perhaps it suffers from the author's blurred or altered purpose. From aiming at a foreign audience, he seems to turn at the end to trying unhappily to jog the American public into a greater sense of responsibility. Evidently Becker felt dissatisfied with his performance. Three years after *The United States* was published Professor Dodd was reassuring him, in effect, that his competence was excellence in anyone else. Dodd added:

I know you and I both became tremendously concerned in the great drama of 1914–1920. I wrote a book that expressed that concern, a sort of contribution to the cause of democracy. You wrote one. I have not seen that you lost your poise at all, although in some chapters of that book you were not as *gründlich* as you were wont to be.[28]

It is significant of the extent to which ideals of detachment and objectivity were Becker's ideals in historical writing after all, that he did not pour out his intense feelings in a really debunking history, which *The United States: An Experiment in Democracy* is not. Instead, during this time of stress, he tried other literary forms. Writing seems to have been to him a more satisfactory and natural means of expression than talking, although many people testify to his occasional conversational brilliance. Suffering as he was from a temporary discontent with history writing, Becker sought another means of expressing the disillusionment he felt.

It was at this time that he most seriously experimented with writing poetry. Apparently almost all writers (and a

[28] William E. Dodd to Becker, March 1, 1923.

surprising number of people in less susceptible profes-
sions) are driven to write verse during acute attacks of
their malady. Only a very few lines of Becker's verse sur-
vived, aside from little jingles to his grandson and other
verses for children. But there is no doubt that Becker tried,
for a time at least, to write more serious poetry. The whole
story, so far as his papers give it, lies in one brief, handwritten letter from Carl Van Doren, dated at Urbana, Illinois:

Your verses have followed me here, where I have been giving
some lectures . . . only after a good deal of delay.

It seems to me that the sonnets suffer from a certain flatness
now and then which leaves one questioning a little whether
prose would not have been better. They have a vibrant irony,
they are correct and strong and they mean a great deal. But
they are excellent verse rather than good poetry in my judgment. Perhaps I would put it better to say that I think three
paragraphs on this saintly vicar would come nearer to doing
his job than three sonnets.

Do I seem very outspoken? It is because I see a pretty genuine satiric gift behind these pieces, which I think you could
afford to indulge.[29]

Since the verses have disappeared, one is free either to
doubt Van Doren's competence in the matter, and thence
to grieve over the loss of the sonnets, or to assume that
he was probably right, and to admire Becker for seeing it
too. Is there not perhaps too much of clarity, too little of
intensity in Becker's writing to indicate a potential poet
in the twentieth-century definition? As E. B. White puts
it: "A poet dares be just so clear and no clearer; he ap-

[29] Carl Van Doren to Becker, March 13, 1922.

Carl Becker

proaches lucid ground warily, like a mariner who is determined not to scrape his bottom on anything solid. A poet's pleasure is to withhold a little of his meaning, to intensify by mystification." [30] Could anything be further removed from the literary ideal to which Becker had devoted himself for over twenty years? Although he might modify or try to abandon his usual canons of writing when he attempted poetry, it seems likely that his poetic intention would still bear more resemblance to John Gay's than to John Donne's. Van Doren's remarks indicate that his performance was also closer to an eighteenth-century ideal than to a seventeenth- or twentieth-century notion of poetry. Are not the virtues ascribed to Becker's sonnets the very ones allowed the Augustans? And is not its disqualifying defect, the very defect of those virtues? Van Doren thought it was prosaic, and to an age in which "a poem should not mean but be," it probably was.

Still, writing poetry may have been a private emotional outlet for Becker all of his life; on the other hand, he may never have written anything but light verse after 1922. In either case he evidently accepted Van Doren's judgment that his proper talent lay in prose.

As for the positive part of Van Doren's advice, Becker was already trying satire. He wrote an allegory of contemporary society in all its aspects, with particular attention to the Paris Peace Conference. Ostensibly a story for children somewhat on the A. A. Milne pattern with a good deal of verse incorporated in the stories, it was called *The King of Beasts*. It is Becker's only completed manuscript of book length that remains unpublished. It

[30] E. B. White, "Unzip the Veil," *The Practical Cogitator* (Boston: Houghton Mifflin, 1945), pp. 472–473.

154

Art of Writing

was rejected by eleven publishers. Again Van Doren wrote frank and direct criticism:

I read it with steady delight in the satire. At the same time, however, I think the story suffers from a lack of dramatic emphasis. That is the narrative element does not stand out with sufficient conspicuousness to carry the thing through. To put it another way, the satire crouches so close to the path of the story that I found myself always peeping at one side or the other for satirical claws and not being sure where I was going along the path. This quality in the book, it seems to me limits the audience more than was needed in the circumstances. As you see, the book is neither simple enough to be read by children without noticing the satire nor adult enough to be read by adults without making them feel that they are stealing something from the children.[31]

Publishers were undoubtedly right in thinking *The King of Beasts* would not sell in 1922; it would be even less publishable today since many of the contemporary allusions would be missed. Another defect—or perhaps another way of stating what Van Doren points out—is that the satire is both too broad and too deep. Too many of man's ways and institutions are attacked; the force is weakened by being divided among almost innumerable targets. All is folly and wickedness. There is naught to choose between "the Beasts that Prey" and those "that Pray." The creatures who live after the word of the Law are fully as cruel as the Lawless, and none are more contemptible than the Lambs who "mean well," but "have soft hearts and like to live in the blessed hope that some day all will be well." [32]

[31] Carl Van Doren to Becker, Jan. 6, 1923.
[32] Becker, *The King of Beasts,* MS.

Carl Becker

Becker was perhaps too hard on himself in feeling that he had lost his poise—after all his *Declaration of Independence* was written in 1922 and his teaching at this time was extremely successful—but *The United States,* the vanished sonnets, and *The King of Beasts* do indicate that the course of his writing was considerably less clear and steady than it had been or than it would be again.

Despite the exceptions, the general rule that most of his work was occasioned by someone else's request or suggestion may be true. That is quite different from saying that it arose out of the requests.

If ideas for some of his best work—like the Benjamin Franklin article in the *Dictionary of American Biography,* or the study of the Declaration of Independence [33] —were directly suggested by editors, other things like *The Heavenly City* and *Progress and Power*—seem to have grown naturally out of his own mind, constantly seeded by reading and fertilized by reflection.[34] Possibly he needed the pressure of an obligation to make him put his work into finished form. If so, he undertook enough to keep himself writing steadily. In his early years at Kansas it was con-

[33] Carl Van Doren to Becker, Jan. 9, 1920.

[34] Alfred North Whitehead's *Science and the Modern World* was particularly suggestive to Becker. His comparison of the Middle Ages as "the age of faith, based upon reason" and the eighteenth century as "the age of reason, based upon faith" (*Science and the Modern World,* p. 80) seems to have been partly responsible for the formulation of the thesis of *The Heavenly City* (Notes, drawer 9). Cf. Becker's list of books which influenced him greatly (*New Republic,* XCVII [Dec. 7, 1938], 135).

An essay by O. Elton, "Love of Fame," *Modern Studies* (London, 1907) may have been the original stimulus that resulted years later in the last chapter of *The Heavenly City*—"*The Uses of Posterity*" (Notes, drawer 9).

stant book reviewing for the *Dial,* the *Nation,* and the *Outlook* that gave him invaluable experience, and which he sought for that reason. Later this was unnecessary and he did reviews only for books of exceptional interest to him. He had standing invitations from the editors of half a dozen journals to write reviews or articles. Toward the end of his life publishers vied for the honor of having a new book of his (or a new collection of old essays) on their lists. He wrote only on what interested him and then only after "exploring with infinite patience every part" [35] of the subject, but he still devoted every morning to writing. He wrote "on demand" only in the sense that everything he wrote was demanded. It is impossible to tell whether books like *Progress and Power* or *The Heavenly City* were written because he was invited to give a series of lectures and had to have something to say, or whether he accepted the invitation because he had something about ready to be said. It is at least plausible to conclude that he simply used some of the many occasions that offered to present lectures or to publish articles that would have been written sooner or later with or without occasion.

These then were the chief rules which Becker found and followed in learning to write—"to have an irrepressible desire to write, to be always reading with discrimination, and to be always writing as well as one can."

There is a tradition at Cornell that Becker once gave another word of advice on writing, and thereby another glimpse of how he wrote himself. A group of graduate students sought him asking what they must do to become good writers. When he told them to go forth and rewrite

[35] "Art of Writing."

everything twelve times, they departed sorrowing. It is easy to believe that Becker himself rewrote everything twelve times and more. There are among his papers as many as six or seven typewritten versions of one article and before that there was undoubtedly a handwritten draft much revised. A few original drafts of articles have been kept, although in general only typewritten manuscripts are in the files. Becker did not compose on the typewriter. His habit seems to have been to write a first draft in longhand—doing a good deal of rewriting as he went along—then to type it (seldom revising as he typed). He altered the typewritten copy in longhand, interlining and writing inserts on new sheets or on the back. The corrected copy was then typed again in whole or in part. This process was repeated over and over until the final draft was sent to the printer, Becker doing his own typing by a swift, two-fingered method. And that final copy was full of corrections too. In spite of all his labor over his writing, his manuscripts always needed a great deal of editing because his spelling, punctuation, and references were rather casual. Becker sent his material off in good time—grateful letters from his publishers show that—but so long as it remained in his hands it was under scrutiny. If he did not "wear his soul threadbare in the search for the better word, the happier phrase, the smoother transition," [36] it can only have been because he enjoyed the search.

This was not quite the whole of his advice nor of his practice, however. For the young writer there are many pitfalls and some of these he pointed out in "The Art of Writing." The "misleading, irrelevant word 'style'" was

[36] Becker, *Declaration of Independence,* p. 195.

the signpost that pointed directly to the deepest pitfalls in Becker's opinion. He believed: "Good style in writing is like happiness in living—something that comes to you, if it comes at all, only if you are preoccupied with something else: if you deliberately go after it you will probably not get it." Moreover, he disliked the word because "it tends to fix the attention on what is superficial and decorative whereas in reality the foundation of good writing is organic structure." The right path then was "to take care of the thought and let the style take care of itself." [37] Let the writer take thought, decide exactly what it is he wishes to convey, and then look for the words which will fully and exactly convey it. That is all he is concerned with. If he does that the style will be "as good as the quality of the thought permits."

The danger lies in thinking of style as a substitute for ideas, or as a cover-up for trite and uninteresting ones.[38] Good style to Becker was never a "succession of felicitous sounds" but always an appropriate expression of an idea which was interesting, subtle, or universal in appeal. His great care to obtain felicitous rather than unpleasing sounds was not a contradiction of this. Pleasant sounds are simply more appropriate because they aid in conveying the idea, while jarring words, however correct, get in the way.

The last way in the world to write well, Becker thought, is to let some "conventional notion of good writing" determine the arrangement of words.[39] The "shape and pressure

[37] Max Lerner to Becker, Dec. 13 [1932?]. "I should like very much to subscribe to your injunction to take care of the thought and let the style take care of itself."

[38] Becker, "Labelling the Historians," *Everyman,* pp. 136–137.

[39] *Ibid.,* p. 137.

of the idea" would determine the form if the writer concentrated on mastering the content—on thinking clearly and logically about the matter rather than the manner. He so far agreed with Henry James, who completely identified form with substance,[40] as to say: "The style, if there is to be any worth mentioning, must wait upon the idea, which is itself form as well as substance." [41] The point of all this, Becker put in a sentence: "Have something of your own to say, and then say it in your own way."

Unlike many who give that advice, he saw fully the difficulties lying in the words "your own."

We are all under a certain pressure, from the social group or profession to which we belong, to think as the group thinks, and to use the clichés the group understands, so that we easily become habituated to certain conventional patterns of thought and stereotyped forms of expression. Anyone who wishes to have something of his own to say and to say it in his own way must avoid, as the sin against the Holy Ghost, these conventional patterns of thought and stereotyped forms of expression.

The wry remarks which follow on the academic stereotype must have been more than half serious. The academic style comes naturally to professors, because they know so much, he explained.

[40] Henry James to Hugh Walpole, May 19, 1912, *Letters of Henry James,* ed. Percy Lubbock (New York: Scribner's, 1920), II, 237, cited by Becker, Notes, drawer 2.

[41] Cf. his introduction to the second edition of *The Declaration of Independence* (New York: Knopf, 1942), p. viii: "It is a favorite notion of mine that in literary discourse form and content are two aspects of the same thing."

Knowing so much, we cannot easily think of any particular thing without thinking at the same time of everything it is related to in heaven and earth; and so the concrete instance, regarded in this broad way, is a nuisance until, divested of all that makes it vivid and alive, we can subsume it in a generalized statement. Aware that there is much to be said on the one hand, and equally much to be said on the other, we feel the need of safeguarding even the simplest affirmation by triple qualifications, remote historical allusions, and parenthetical cross references.

The dreadful necessity of leaving out everything except what is strictly relevant was one he accepted early and commended to his students, but he saw that the generality of scholars had not screwed their courage up so far.

But more dangerous than any professional stereotype, after all, are the pervasive, inconspicuous literary stereotypes. Every reader has his mind filled with them; they are not in themselves unlovely like the jargon of the lawyer, the business man, or the social scientist, but the predominance of them in anyone's writing gives it "a borrowed excellence" which quite deprives it of character. Avoiding them is difficult; Becker can only say try not to use them. "Try to understand clearly what you yourself . . . know or think or feel about the subject, and then express it in a form of words that is natural to you." If the style is then not very good, it cannot be improved by "borrowed mannerisms" and "tricks of the trade," but only by becoming better yourself through "working, reading, observing, thinking honestly, and becoming absorbed in things more important than oneself."

With that final caution, Becker ended his remarks on

the art of writing. Most of the counsel given there could be inferred from scattered comments in his published writings. For example, the major tenet of his creed—be yourself—is implied in his chapter on "The Literary Qualities of the Declaration." The only large defect he saw in the original draft of the Declaration of Independence came from Jefferson's violation of that principle. In the paragraph against slavery, which Congress deleted, Jefferson had tried to adopt a tone that was unnatural to him, Becker believed. The lines rang false because Jefferson himself had not the temperament to sustain "the grand manner" with sincerity. He had not a "profoundly emotional apprehension of experience" and so his "vehement philippic against negro slavery" (as John Adams called it) is not moving as it was meant to be. Becker did not doubt that Jefferson "apprehended the injustice of slavery"; that Jefferson felt it deeply he did doubt.[42] In other parts of the Declaration, the appeal is to the mind and not the heart, and Jefferson was at his best, but in the slavery charge he felt called upon "to stir the reader's emotions, to make him feel a righteous indignation at the king's acts, a profound contempt for the man and his motives." [43] He could not do it:

We remain calm in reading it because Jefferson, one cannot but think, remained calm in writing it. For want of phrases charged with deep feeling, he resorts to italics, vainly endeavoring to stir the reader by capitalizing and underlining the words that need to be stressed—a futile device which serves only to accentuate the sense of artifice and effort.[44]

[42] *Declaration of Independence*, p. 221.   [43] *Ibid.*, p. 214.
[44] *Ibid.*, pp. 220–221.

The style must suit the man as well as the subject, for it will inevitably reflect him for better or for worse. This conviction was a fertile theme for Becker, as well as a rule of writing. His comments about George Bancroft's historical writing [45] and far more his brief analysis of Benjamin Franklin's prose [46] illuminate the men as well. But this chapter on the author of the Declaration is surely a supreme example of brilliant literary criticism combined with psychological intuition. Our interest in it is intensified by the peculiar affinity between the minds of Jefferson and Becker. One cannot help thinking that the historian who was no lecturer had felt with the statesman who was no orator that overwhelming desire when speaking to "cross out what he has just said and say it over again in a different way." [47] Becker also clearly felt Jefferson's distress at the "depredations" committed by Congress upon his carefully composed document. Further, Becker's friends saw, and he admitted to one of them, that he examined what he felt to be a limitation of his own writing when he explained Jefferson's inability to achieve the grand manner.[48] Since he was more introspective than Jefferson, he had decided that he lacked a "profoundly passionate nature" and he eschewed any attempt to write in tones of deep emotion. He might have said with Wordsworth:

> The moving accident is not my trade,
> To freeze the blood I have no ready Arts.

[45] *Everyman,* pp. 132–142.
[46] Becker, "Benjamin Franklin," *DAB,* VI, 597.
[47] *Declaration of Independence,* p. 195.
[48] Sabine, *op. cit.,* p. ix; Hawke, *op. cit.,* p. 34.

Carl Becker

Like Wordsworth and Jefferson, he spoke to "thinking hearts." And so he wrote not about manning the barricades, but about revolutions in men's minds.

Becker's literary virtues, although of a lesser order, lay in the same direction as Jefferson's. Like Jefferson's writing Becker's too had "elevation" though it did not have the "massive strength" of the grand manner. Becker's words in defense of democratic virtues, penned during the years when democracy seemed most in peril, resemble the Declaration of Independence far more than they resemble contemporaneous words of Winston Churchill's.

To have faith in the dignity and worth of the individual man as an end in himself, to believe that it is better to be governed by persuasion than by coercion, to believe that fraternal good will is more worthy than a selfish and contentious spirit, to believe that in the long run all values are inseparable from the love of truth and the disinterested search for it, to believe that knowledge and the power it confers should be used to promote the welfare and happiness of all men rather than to serve the interests of those individuals and classes whom fortune and intelligence endow with temporary advantage—these are the values which are affirmed by the traditional democratic ideology. But they are older and more universal than democracy and do not depend upon it. . . . They are the values that readily lend themselves to rational justification, yet need no justification.[49]

If these lines fall short of the grand manner, it is because, like the Declaration, they do not have "unsophisticated directness" or the "effect of passion restrained." They carry

[49] *New Liberties for Old*, pp. 149–150.

Art of Writing

conviction, but they do not bring the surge of emotion that comes with Churchill's words:

The battle of Britain is about to begin. Upon this battle depends the survival of Christian civilisation. Upon it depends our own British life and the long continuity of our institutions and our Empire. The whole fury and might of the enemy must very soon be turned on us. Hitler knows that he will have to break us in this island or lose the war. If we can stand up to him all Europe may be free, and the life of the world may move forward into broad, sunlit uplands; but if we fail then the whole world, including the United States, and all that we have known and cared for, will sink into the abyss of a new dark age made more sinister, and perhaps more prolonged, by the lights of perverted science. Let us therefore brace ourselves to our duty and so bear ourselves that if the British Commonwealth and Empire lasts for a thousand years men will still say, "This was their finest hour." [50]

Of course Becker was not, as Churchill was, exhorting a people "to dare and to endure," but he was doing what his talents better fitted him for—persuading a people to think well that they might know their heritage was worth preserving.

For this task of the last five years of his life, Becker wrote the most straightforward, earnest prose that he ever produced. There is little of the delicate irony that pervades *The Heavenly City* in *How New Will the Better World Be?* That was sacrificed, one feels, because it would not help to "obtain the end of the writer"—which was clearly to infuse political concern, judgment, and sophistication into as many people as possible. Once he set out to

[50] Speech to the House of Commons, June 18, 1940, *Parliamentary Debates* (5th ser.), 362 (London: H.M. Stationery Office, 1940), 60–61.

persuade, Becker could insinuate enlightened views into all sorts of minds—even closed ones—as blandly as ever Benjamin Franklin could. His was not the job of rousing men to fight for democracy, but only to think more clearly about it before it was too late. Still, to do that he had to take his place with the believers, and the skepticism of his days of contemplation, however mellow, had to be put by for less critical times. Sufficient faith for the task he had, and he had it "at the expense of some painful travail of the spirit" after much "reflection upon the enigma of existence." [51] Here the twentieth-century historian parts company with his eighteenth-century model. For Becker, even before 1918, there was none of that "complacent optimism" that Jefferson enjoyed.

Both men put their faith in reason and democracy— Jefferson believing that they had placed all human ills and imperfections in the course of ultimate extinction, Becker believing only that, faulty as they were, their abandonment would bring down the long night of barbarism. Jefferson's optimism was limitless and glowing. Becker's bleak remnant of optimism was almost negative —little more than, with Justice Holmes, *not* believing in sudden ruin.

However strongly Becker's peculiar felicities may remind us of Jefferson's, his mood and tone are anything but Jeffersonian. Although Jefferson's values were Becker's too, their views of how those values fit into the universe were vastly different. Jefferson depicts a world of Newtonian order; Becker a chaos of whirling forces. But both wielded "masterly pens" and both did so by dint of careful labor.

[51] *Declaration of Independence*, pp. 218–219.

V

The Practice of Writing

One whose ear is sensitive to the subtler, elusive harmonies of expression, one who in imagination hears the pitch and cadence and rhythm of the thing he wishes to say before he says it, often makes a sad business of public speaking. . . . He instinctively wishes to cross out what he has just said, and say it over again in a different way. . . . In writing he can cross out and rewrite at leisure, as often as he likes, until the sound and the sense are perfectly suited—until the thing composes.[1]

ONE of the few handwritten first drafts which remains in Becker's files is a part of Chapter V of his *Eve of the Revolution*. This particular chapter, "A Little Discreet Conduct," is a model of Becker's literary virtues; it shows to the full the happy perfection that can occasionally be attained in the construction of a chapter. It is unified and coherent; it flows from paragraph to paragraph through faultless transitions. This chapter exhibits at once Becker's chief interest in history and his greatest historical

[1] Becker, *Declaration of Independence*, p. 195.

gifts. In a letter to William E. Dodd in 1920, Becker indicated his theme:

The conclusion I draw [from the World War, 1914–1918] is not that the world is divided into good men and bad, intelligent and ignorant, and that all will be well when the bad men are circumvented and the ignorant are enlightened. This old eighteenth century view is too naive and simple. Neither good men nor bad wanted *this* war . . . yet neither were able to prevent it. . . . For good men and bad, ignorant and enlightened (even as enlightened as Mr. Wilson), reason and aspiration and emotion—what we call principles, faith, ideals —are without their knowing it at the service of complex and subtle instinctive reactions and impulses. This is the meaning, if it has any, of my book on the Eve of the Revolution, and particularly of the chapter on Adams and Hutchinson.[2]

"A Little Discreet Conduct" is chiefly a portrayal of the fateful lack of discreet conduct on the part of two men—Thomas Hutchinson and Samuel Adams. The brilliant contrast Becker drew between these two men of Massachusetts illuminates the path to revolution during the relatively quiet years between the Boston Massacre and the Boston Tea Party. Becker later wrote the studies of Adams and Hutchinson for the *Dictionary of American Biography,* expanding and developing his analysis of the relations between the two men a good deal further, but both biographies are outlined in this chapter.

In *The Eve of the Revolution,* which conveys "not a record of what men did, but a sense of how they thought and felt about what they did," [3] Becker disclaimed any attempt at writing orthodox history based entirely on

[2] Becker to Dodd, June 17, 1920.
[3] *Eve of the Revolution,* p. vii.

Practice of Writing

verifiable references. But the scholarly authority behind the book was recognized at once, even though at that time (1918) "scientific history" was a great deal more attempted and more honored than it is today. Perhaps critics were disarmed by Becker's own genial admission that the book might not be history, but they would not have been so disarmed if "the illusion of the intellectual atmosphere of past time" had not been utterly convincing.[4]

The "reproduction of the thought and feeling" of past days had the ring of truth to the scholar and the expert not less than to the uninitiated.[5] It had it, I think, because after knowledge of documents left off, Becker used "those fainter powers of apprehension and surmise and sensitiveness, by which after all, most high truth has been reached as well as most high art and poetry." [6] Still, a look into his files—and even more into his doctoral dissertation —shows that behind the "rather free paraphrase of what some imagined spectator or participant might have thought or said" [7] lay an immense detailed knowledge of what, in fact, a great many actual persons had said and written. Becker's thesis, *The History of Political Parties in the Province of New York, 1760–1776,* was a thoroughly documented, scholarly study of the formation of revolutionary parties. He was absorbed in the mental processes by which the revolutionist was gradually differentiated from the loyalist. For this study he read a vast amount of primary source material on the first phase of the revolution

[4] *Ibid.,* pp. vii–viii.
[5] Cf. review by C. H. Van Tyne, *AHR,* XXIV, 734–735.
[6] Gilbert Murray, *Five Stages of Greek Religion* (Oxford, 1925), p. 206.
[7] *Eve of the Revolution,* p. vii.

—letters, diaries, newspapers, minutes of committee meetings, and pamphlets. Unfortunately the notes for this study are not now in the Becker files. The only large collection of research notes on American history remaining is the set done for his book *The Beginnings of the American People*. The reading Becker did for his first two books gave him an intimate acquaintance with men and ideas in the last half of the eighteenth century in America and in England. Information he had in quantity; *The Eve of the Revolution* is evidently the result of recollecting it in tranquillity after years in which his memory had performed the sure task of sifting and selecting from the mass of facts those most vivid and meaningful to Carl Becker. It added something new to the history of the American Revolution, not because it was an "original contribution to knowledge," but because it was a unique interpretation of old facts. Not a competent organization of 3 by 5 slips, but the creation of individual imagination, which therefore had to be new. "Be yourself; it is the only thing nobody else can be" was a rule for writing history as well as anything else.

So completely was *The Eve* a presentation of what interested Carl Becker in 1918 about the years from 1763 to 1776 that in the original draft it did not include (or only barely mentioned) such famous and stirring events as the Stamp Act Congress, the Boston Massacre, and the battles of Lexington and Concord. Descriptions of these were added on the request of the editor of the series who thought that the readers who expected these things ought not to be disappointed.[8] The book is about events in the minds of men, not overt actions, for the most part.

[8] Allen Johnson to Carl Becker, March 15, 1918.

Practice of Writing

Although Chapter V presents most effectively the thoughts and feelings of Samuel Adams and Thomas Hutchinson, neither of these character sketches brings out any new facts or corrects any previous study. For Hutchinson, at least, Becker apparently relied entirely on secondary sources. The quotations from Hutchinson's letters are almost entirely taken from those quoted in James K. Hosmer's *Life of Thomas Hutchinson*.[9] Becker did not set out to correct Hosmer; he accepted his work, but he refocused it. Not by research but by reflection, by bringing his acute imagination to bear upon the old, well-known facts of the colonial governor's career Becker was able to bring him to life in a portrait that is intensely human and poignant. The struggle between the governor, who "possessed the efficient mind" but was often wrong-headed, and the "Great Incendiary," who "had the soul of a Jacobin," is as gripping as a novel because it is told with as much artistry.

His first concern—and this is in accord with the rules he worked out for himself—was to get clear organization. His transitions linked paragraph to paragraph, chapter to chapter, so firmly that the whole is a faultless chain—perfectly distinguishable, link from link, yet unbroken. Chapter V of *The Eve of the Revolution* is a superb example of his technique. The quotations at the head of the chapter form the prelude:

[9] James K. Hosmer, *Life of Thomas Hutchinson* (Boston: Houghton Mifflin, 1896). Becker's notes and the MS of the *Eve of the Revolution* show this. Becker read the unpublished Hutchinson papers before writing the *DAB* article (see his Notes, drawer 16) but not before writing *The Eve*. He also used P. O. Hutchinson's *Diary and Letters of Thomas Hutchinson* (2 vols.; Boston: Houghton Mifflin, 1884–86).

It has been his [Thomas Hutchinson's] principle from a boy that mankind are to be governed by the discerning few, and it has been ever since his ambition to be the hero of the few.—Samuel Adams.

We have not been so quiet these five years. . . . If it were not for two or three Adamses, we should do well enough.—Thomas Hutchinson.[10]

These quotations are precisely suitable because they not only show the deep gulf between Adams and Hutchinson, but they also are fairer remarks than they usually made about each other and they forecast very well Becker's own judgment of each man. Each said much more violent things about the other at times, but Becker did not seek merely vivid contrasts; he was introducing strains that would be developed further.

The first paragraph states the theme. He shows that things were indeed quiet; Horace Walpole thought in December, 1771, that all the storms were happily blown over; and the Connecticut agent, Mr. Johnson, wrote to Wedderburn in October, 1771: "A little discreet conduct on both sides would perfectly reestablish that warm affection and respect toward Great Britain for which this country was once remarkable."

Still, that affection had been strained and we are reminded that "Discreet conduct was nowhere more necessary than in Massachusetts." The deliberate mention, one by one, of a few of the chief men of the colony reveals why that was so: John Adams, James Otis, John Hancock, Governor Francis Bernard, and, above all, Samuel Adams and Thomas Hutchinson.

The third paragraph begins the sketch of Samuel

[10] *Eve of the Revolution,* p. 150.

Adams, which continues through eleven pages to the point where the sketch of Hutchinson begins. Since the first draft of the chapter is fragmentary up to the beginning of the description of Thomas Hutchinson, let us begin a comparison of the rough draft and the printed version at this point. The closing paragraph of the Adams sketch ends with this sentence: "Of all these restless adversaries and infamous plotters of ruin, the chief in the mind of Samuel Adams, was probably Mr. Thomas Hutchinson."

Beginning there the rough draft reads:

Judged only by what he said and did, and by such other superficial sources of information as are open to the historian, Mr. Th. Hutchinson does not appear to have been, at any time in his life, an Enemy of the Human Race.

The final version is:

Judged only by what he did and said and by such other sources of information as are open to the historian, Thomas Hutchinson does not appear to have been, prior to 1771, an Enemy of the Human Race.

There are four changes in this sentence—each one attesting to the care and sensitivity with which Becker's revisions were made. First, the order is reversed from the hackneyed "said and did" to "did and said"; after all, by any pragmatic test a man's actions rank ahead of his words. Second, the "superficial" is omitted. Besides other possible objections, it made the line too sibilant. Third, the "Mr." is dropped because it repeated the "Mr. Thomas Hutchinson" of the previous sentence, and this was particularly undesirable because there it carried the sneering tones of Samuel Adams. The last and greatest improvement was changing "at any time in his life" to "prior to 1771." The irony is sharpened by dry accuracy.

None of these changes is indicated on the original draft. All were made in some intermediate copy or (more likely) copies which are no longer in his files. This original draft, like all the others, indicates that Becker wrote "with ease and rapidity," no more "constructing his sentences with slow and painful effort" than Jefferson did.[11] There are many changes, crossed out words and slashed out paragraphs, but signs of really difficult writing are absent. There are few places where repeated false starts to a sentence appear; crossed out lines never fill up more space on the page than accepted lines. There are no indications that he was ever simply stuck and unable to get going. His words run together as if they flowed from a flying pen seldom lifted from the paper. Becker made endless changes: substituting the more exact word for the less, the simpler statement for the more complex, one word where there had been two before; revising always away from the conventional, the stereotyped, the pretentious; but his original drafts (by 1918 at least) were not crude productions as they stood. His original sentences have all the characteristic flavor. Where whole sentences or paragraphs are crossed out, it is usually done to change or clarify the organization or to compress a thought by omitting details.

His characterization of Hutchinson completes the statement of the main theme of the chapter: an unaccustomed quiet prevailed in the colonies even in Massachusetts; if it could be prolonged and deepened the colonies would be saved for the empire, but some powerful forces were

[11] *Declaration of Independence,* p. 198.

making for dissension. It was not yet clear which would triumph. Then Adams and Hutchinson are shown as the principals—two determined men out to build inconsistent worlds. We see then that they do not wish to compromise and do not know how.

The climax of the book is here, in the middle of chapter five. Suspense is turned into premonition in one crucial paragraph. Structurally this paragraph forms the link between the long flashback portrayals of Adams and Hutchinson and the continuing narrative. A transition paragraph both in form and in emotional tone, it represents Becker's most painstaking work. Seldom indeed, if the evidence of his few remaining first drafts be taken as typical, did Becker labor so long to perfect one small section. It is interesting to see how he brought it, bit by bit, to its final shape.

The organization must have been perfectly clear in his mind from the beginning: from the first draft to the printed copy the position of this paragraph was not changed, nor the general burden of it. It developed one clear idea: the reconciliation which seemed to be in the offing in 1771 was not going to come because Adams and Hutchinson were fated to keep on widening the breach instead of narrowing it. Becker's tragic sense of life and of history became almost explicit here. The war came not because of the actions of bad men, but because "for good men and bad, ignorant and enlightened . . . reason and aspiration and emotion—what we call principles, faith, ideals—are without their knowing it at the service of complex and subtle instinctive reactions and impulses." [12] Knowing as deeply as any poet that "words have an aura

[12] Becker to Dodd, June 17, 1920.

as well as a core," [13] he kept rewriting until his meaning was conveyed in the very pitch and cadence of the words, until the reader could hear in the distance the slow, sure step of impending doom. Succeeding paragraphs then would detail how Adams and Hutchinson between them brought about the final break.

The Hutchinson sketch closed with a letter the governor wrote denouncing Samuel Adams as a "Great Incendiary." In one paragraph Becker wanted to bring us back to the line of marching events and at the same time let us see where that line must end. This was his first attempt:

FIRST DRAFT—A

The letter undirected and undated, in which ~~Gov~~ Th. H. pronounced this judgment of S. Adams, was probably written about the time ~~when he~~ of his accession to the governorship; about the time, that is to say when Mr. Johnson was writing to Wedderburn that "a little discreet conduct on both sides would perfectly reestablish that warm aff. & respect for Gt. B for which this country was once remarkable." This was no doubt true advice, and perhaps practicable to follow, on both sides, so far as both sides were on opposite sides of the Atlantic. Lord North did not irritate John Adams and John Adams ~~was~~ not being ~~the daily companion of the minister~~ was
a member of the House

[13] Joseph Wood Krutch, "The Indispensable Century," *Saturday Review of Literature*, XXXIII (Sept. 2, 1950), 7.

not a persistent thorn in ~~his~~ the side of the first minister. ~~With~~

~~M In the case of Mr. H and S Adams it was otherwise different~~.

These men might grow ~~tired of controversy & be willing~~

weary of altercations, and willingly let the controversy sub-

side. In the case of Mr. H. & Samuel Adams, it was not so.
They were on opposite sides to be sure; but of necessity
~~They~~ lived together in the little town of Boston, were ~~brought~~

                    the performance of
bound to come together in virtue of official functions, & ~~were~~
come face to face round the corner in some or other
likely any day to ~~meet in the~~ narrow streets. ~~In the case of S.~~

~~Adams and Mr. H~~. Under these circumstances, & each hold-
                both
          ~~neither~~ xxxx [illegible] xxxx Human Race
ing so low an opinion of the other's honesty, a little discreet

conduct, even a very little, was scarcely to be looked for from

~~Sam~~ Samuel Adams or Mr. Hutchinson. And in fact both men,

during the years 1771 & 1772 when if ever there was a prospect

that the controversy would subside, did what they could to

perpetuate it: wittingly or unwittingly they ~~did their~~ labored

to push the continent into a rebellion, giving and taking oc-

casion to recall ancient grudges, to renew useless ~~arguments~~

debates, daily keeping the dying embers alive against the time

when some chance wind might blow them to a devouring

flame.

Notice how the logical sequence from paragraph to paragraph was provided in this first draft. The beginning and ending of this passage remained the same except for slight verbal changes through every revision. Nevertheless, much of the passage as it stands is awkward and overwritten, and it comforts us to see that even Becker had to fight those ubiquitous and meaningless "in the case of's." Not satisfied with the sound of it, Becker reached for a clean sheet of paper and tried rewriting the last third: [14]

SECOND DRAFT—B

~~his Enemy & the chief Enemy~~ and each holding so low an opinion of the other's honesty,—under these circumstances, discreet conduct, even a little, was scarcely to be looked for. ~~Under the circumstances No conduct on the part of either man could be thought of as discreet on the pa by the other.~~
                                                wittingly or unwittingly
Both men, in fact, did what they could, during the ~~two years~~ 1771 and 1772, to ~~keep the great controversy alive, to perpetuate that~~ perpetuate the quarrel, giving & taking occasion ~~to renew useless arguments~~ to recall ~~old grudges~~ ancient differences & renew useless arguments, keeping as it were the

[14] My assumption has been that Becker wrote all the drafts given here (A-D) at one sitting and that a final revision (or more than one) was made before the book was printed. It is possible, however, that Becker did each one at a separate sitting with considerable time in between.

dying embers alive against the time when some chance wind might blow them once more into devouring flame.

Although he rearranged the last two sentences several times, he still failed to achieve what he was after, so he slashed it out, turned the sheet over and rewrote the paragraph entirely:

THIRD DRAFT—C

The letter, undated and undirected, in which Th H pronounced this deliberate judgment of S Adams, was probably written about the time of his accession to the Governorship; about the time, that is to say, when Mr. Johnson, the Conn Agent, was writing to Wedderburn that a "little discreet conduct on both sides" would ~~fully re-establish~~ restore the former cordial relations between Gt. B & the colonies. This was not good advice, and perhaps practicable to be followed, "on both sides," so far as ~~both sides~~. the parties to the controversy were ~~sufficiently~~ in a physical sense, sufficiently separated. ~~Lord~~ Lord North did not irritate John Adams, at least not excessively; and John Adams, not ~~be present daily~~ being in daily attendance in the House of Commons, on the opposition benches, was not a persistent thorn in the side of the first
official

179

Minister. These men and perhaps even Mr. Wedderburn himself, might have grown weary of altercations carried on ~~at a~~
so great disadvantages
under
~~distance of 3000 miles~~ & without the stimulus of mutual re-

ciprocal exasperation ~~engendered~~ engendered by reasonable
therefore
propinquity: ~~These men~~ might conceivably have let the con-

troversy subside. But Samuel Adams & Mr. H. were differently

situated. Both men, unfortunately, lived in Boston, which was

~~not a~~ smaller then, and in some ways more provincial, than

it is now: necessarily, ~~requirements of the perform~~ in the

performance of official functions, their ~~conflicting~~ keen & in-

comparable [*sic*] minds were brought to bear upon ~~matters~~

the same matters: & they were likely, any day, to come face

to face round the corner in some or other narrow street. From

S. Adams & Th H, seeing that neither had a high opinion of

the other's honesty a "little discreet conduct," even a very

little, was scarcely to be looked for under the circumstances.

—And in fact both men, during the years 1771 & 1772, when
good
if ever there was ~~a~~ prospect that the controv. might subside,

did what they could to perpetuate it. Giving & taking occasion

to ~~keep~~ recall ancient grudges or renew useless debates, and

so during those calm days keeping the dying embers alive

180

against the time when some chance wind might fan them into devouring flames.

The first thing he did in this third draft was to shorten the quotation from Johnson's letter giving just enough to recall the passage cited earlier with the key phrase "a little discreet conduct." The sentence, already a long one, was thus simplified and improved. The first real difficulty was tackled in the next five sentences where he had repeatedly used the word *side* or *sides*. To be sure, the sentences were intelligible enough upon a careful reading, but the repetition of "both sides" . . . "both sides," . . . "opposite sides" . . . "thorn in the side" . . . "subside" . . . "opposite sides" did not come off as a device for emphasis and without that it was merely flat or even confusing. After this was smoothed out, a number of small changes were made through the rest of the paragraph, and some of the phrases introduced in draft B were incorporated.

After that, Becker evidently reread this third draft (C) testing its clarity and cogency. Anything which confused or blurred the main point had to be eliminated. I think that was the reason for his subsequent dropping of the lines about Lord North and John Adams. These lines made a colorful illustration of his point, one which intrigues the imagination. Too much so, perhaps. It conjures up pictures of persons and situations that are not properly a part of this particular tale and is more distracting than helpful. Moreover, it breaks the passage in two distinct halves which might well have been two separate paragraphs—the first ending with "might conceivably have let the controversy subside"; the second beginning: "But Samuel Adams and Mr. Hutchinson were differently situated." By the omission of the two sentences on North and John Adams, in spite of the nice contrast they made with Hutchinson and Sam Adams, the unity of the paragraph was preserved and the structure tightened:

FOURTH DRAFT—D

The letter, undated & undirected, in which ~~Mr. H~~ Th H pronounced this deliberate judgment of S. Adams, was probably written about the time of his accession to the Governorship; that is to say, about the time when Mr. Johnson, the Conn. agent, was writing to W- that "A little discreet conduct on both sides" would perfectly restore cordial relations between

In the way of

~~Eng~~. B. & her colonies. ~~Of~~ discreet conduct, even a very little,

~~either~~

not much was to be ~~exp~~ hoped from Governor H or S Adams in their dealings with each other; ~~seeing that they each had~~ ~~so low an opinion of the other's honesty.~~ Unfortunately, they had dealings with each other; their incomparable minds were necessarily, in the performance of official functions, brought to bear on the same matters & ~~personally they were likely, any~~ ~~day~~ Unfortunately they both lived in ~~Boston the small town~~ ~~of~~ Boston, and were likely, any day, to come face to face round the corner of some or other narrow street of that small town. ~~Each~~ The ~~stimulus of~~ reciprocal exasperation engendered by reasonable propinquity, so necessary to the maintenance of ~~perpetual~~ altercations, was a perpetual stimulus to both men, confirming each in his low opinion of the others honesty of purpose. And therefore, both men, preeminent as leaders on either side, did what they could during the years 1771 and 1772, when if ever ~~there was good prospect~~ it appeared that others were "growing weary of altercations," to perpetuate the controversy: by giving and taking occasion to recall ancient grudges or revive fruitless ~~debate~~ disputes, they managed ~~to keep~~ during this time of calm to keep the dying embers alive against the day when some ~~chance~~ rising wind might blow them into a devouring flame.

Whatever was irrelevant was omitted, even when it was only a trifling matter of a short clause like the one about eighteenth-century Boston, which was "smaller, and in some ways more provincial, than it is now." The smallness of Boston in 1771 was relevant to the point he was making; the provinciality of Boston, then or subsequently, was, alas, not relevant and so that part was suppressed.

The change in the last sentence from "some chance wind" to "some rising wind" was really admirable. With one word we are reminded that the wind, however low it gets, never dies. It is inevitable, not a chance, that it will blow again, and the embers of disaffection kept alive by Samuel Adams will flame into rebellion.

Draft D is close to the final form of the paragraph as it appears on pages 175–177 of *The Eve of the Revolution,* but some more changes were made in later revisions which are not now among the Becker Papers. Perhaps the most noticeably unsatisfactory spot remaining in the fourth draft was the phrase "their incomparable minds." "Incomparable" was first substituted for "conflicting" in draft C; it stayed in draft D, although such an ambiguous word must have been only a makeshift until the right word came to mind. Or possibly Becker really wished to use the word in its primary sense—"impossible of comparison" —and only gave it up reluctantly after reflecting that the derived meaning of "fine beyond comparison" has become so much more common that he could not escape it. Several other phrases were not quite satisfactory either. For example, "preeminent as leaders on either side" is awkward. These and other flaws, discernible, perhaps, only to Becker's sensitive ear, disappeared in the final version:

The letter, undated and undirected, in which Thomas Hutchinson pronounced this deliberate judgment on Samuel Adams, was probably written about the time of his accession to the Governorship; that is to say, about the time when Mr. Johnson, the Connecticut Agent, was writing to Wedderburn that "the people seem to grow weary of altercations," and that "a little discreet conduct on both sides" would perfectly restore cordial relations between Britain and her colonies. In the way of "a little discreet conduct," even a very little, not much was to be hoped for from either Governor Hutchinson or Samuel Adams in their dealings with each other. Unfortunately, they *had* dealings with each other: in the performance of official functions, their incommensurable and repellent minds were necessarily brought to bear upon the same matters of public concern. Both, unfortunately, lived in Boston and were likely any day to come face to face round the corner of some or other narrow street of that small town. That reciprocal exasperation engendered by reasonable propinquity, so essential to the life of altercations, was therefore a perpetual stimulus to both men, confirming each in his obstinate opinion of the other as a malicious and dangerous enemy of all that men hold dear. Thus it was that during the years 1771 and 1772, when if ever it appeared that others were "growing weary of altercations," these honorable men and trusted leaders did what they could to perpetuate the controversy. By giving or taking occasion to recall ancient grudges or revive fruitless disputes, wittingly or unwittingly they together managed during this time of calm to keep the dying embers alive against the day when some rising wind might blow them into devouring flames.[15]

The first difference between draft D and the printed version is in the quotation from Johnson. In the final reading the first part of the quotation—"the people seem to grow weary of altercations," is included. This balances the paragraph more perfectly, and is needed as a reminder that Adams and Hutchinson were at that moment somewhat out of step with many of their contemporaries. The next change—inserting the words "a little" into the beginning of the second sentence: "In the way of 'a little discreet conduct' "—is typical of Becker's careful attention to emphasis.

Two small additions follow—"either" is inserted before

[15] *Eve of the Revolution*, pp. 175–177.

Governor Hutchinson in the same sentence, and "had" is italicized in the following one. Italics seem desirable and justifiable in that place, but italics were rarely used by Becker. He used them here purely for emphasis and not to try to rouse the reader's emotions, of course, which was the use he deprecated so strongly in Jefferson's "philippic against slavery." [16]

The next notable alteration occurs in the same sentence. The semicolon after "Unfortunately, they had dealings with each other;" was changed to a colon—a common (in fact a highly characteristic) construction in Becker's writing. Typically the rest of the sentence illustrates, explains, and makes specific the general statement preceding the colon. Here he made another improvement by transposing the phrase "in the performance of official functions" to stand ahead of the main clause instead of in the middle of it, where it separated subject from verb. Then for the ambiguous word "incomparable" he has happily substituted the clear and precise words "incommensurable and repellent." So the sentence reads finally: "Unfortunately, they *had* dealings with each other: in the performance of official functions, their incommensurable and repellent minds were necessarily brought to bear upon the same matters of public concern."

Several one-word changes follow. "Life" for "maintenance" improves that irritating sentence which begins "The reciprocal exasperation engendered by reasonable propinquity . . ." (though, to my mind, it remains too irritating for its worth as onomatopoeia). Then comes another change worth noting. Draft D reads "confirming each in his low opinion of the other's honesty of purpose."

[16] *Declaration of Independence*, pp. 220–221.

See how much better the final version is: "confirming each in his obstinate opinion of the other as a malicious and dangerous enemy of all that men hold dear."

Most interesting of all, perhaps, is the revision of the last sentence of draft D, which becomes two sentences in the final reading. First, it becomes much more sonorous by being put into indirect construction. The opening "Thus it was that" reminds us of the Biblical "And so it came to pass that." Then again the adverbial clause "during the years 1771 and 1772, when if ever it appeared that others were 'growing weary of altercations'" is transposed so that the subject and verb stand together. The subject, by an inspired change, from "both men, preeminent as leaders on either side" becomes "These honorable men and trusted leaders." The connotations of "these honorable men" are grim and full of tragedy for us, though we find in the next paragraph that Samuel Adams openly wished to make "Brutuses of the men of Boston." The last sentence continues the somber rhythm, the falling cadence which tells us as clearly as the words themselves that there will be not peace but a sword.

It remained for the rest of the chapter to show how Adams and Hutchinson dealt with each other, how Adams (conscientiously) and Hutchinson (in the vain endeavor to say the last word) kept the quarrel going. Becker has prepared us to understand why they act as they do and to appreciate at once how each man's action will affect the other and ultimately will affect the relations between Great Britain and the colonies. In this chapter "even the blind can see the two countries drifting into war," [17] William E. Dodd wrote to Becker.

[17] Dodd to Becker, Jan. 23, 1919.

Carl Becker

What was more important from Becker's point of view, they can see why. "This is precisely the task of the historian, to explain why," Becker protested in an exasperated note on Madelin's treatment of the fall of the Bastille.[18] Madelin, instead of explaining why the fall of the Bastille became a great event, treats it as a sham. "This is not writing history, it is merely complaining about the way things happen in history," Becker commented. Given a somewhat similar situation in the affair of the Hutchinson letters, he does not treat it that way. He explains with delicious irony just how it was that Samuel Adams made the publication of the letters into an exposé that ended the governor's influence on his countrymen forever, and how Adams did it in spite of the fact, bewildering to the logical governor, that "in these letters there was no statement of fact or expression of opinion not already well known."[19] Becker's closing paragraph on the letter incident is a typical example of his work. Here he was doing what he thought was his proper task, explaining how a mere affair of words (and not very amazing ones either) had become a great event:

His Majesty did not remove Mr. Hutchinson; but the Governor's usefulness, from every point of view, was at an end. When the notorious letters were finally printed, it appeared that there were seventeen in all, of which six were written by Mr. Hutchinson in the years 1768 and 1769. These latter documents did not in fact add anything to the world's stock of knowledge; but they had been so heralded, ushered in with so much portentous explication that they scarcely needed to

[18] Louis Madelin, *The French Revolution* (New York: Putnam, 1916), p. 85. Cited in Becker's Notes, box 2.
[19] *Eve of the Revolution*, p. 195.

Practice of Writing

be read to be understood. "Had they been Chevy Chase," the Governor said, the people would have believed them "full of evil and treason." It was indeed the perfect fruit of Samuel Adams's labors that the significance of Mr. Hutchinson's letters had in some manner become independent of their contents. So awake were the people to the danger of being deceived, that whatever the Governor now said or ever had written was taken to be but the substance of things hoped for, the evidence of things not seen.[20]

Becker saw that Samuel Adams' great undertaking was to create a climate of opinion in which any loyally conservative crown officer would be judged an Enemy of the Human Race. Hence, for Becker, the victory of the Great Incendiary was proved, not in December, 1773, when the mob at his signal boarded the East India Company's ships and threw tea worth £14,000 into the Boston harbor, but six months earlier, when the men of Boston read treason in their governor's letters. Accordingly Becker spent six pages on the letter episode, "the perfect fruit of Samuel Adams' labors," and disposed of the Tea Party, a far more tangible fruit of his labors, in a dozen lines.[21]

After the affair of the governor's letters, the duel between Adams and Hutchinson was really over; the time when discreet conduct might have counted was past. Becker swiftly brought his chapter to a close, without even mentioning Hutchinson's last indiscretion, his refusal of return clearance papers to the tea ships, which precipitated the final train of crises. By that time it did not matter who did it, Becker implies. A final revealing glimpse of Hutchinson ends the chapter:

[20] *Ibid.*, p. 198.   [21] *Ibid.*, pp. 199, 206.

189

Carl Becker

It was a limitation of Thomas Hutchinson's excellent administrative mind that he was wholly unaware of this crisis. In February of the next year, finding that "a little discreet conduct," or indeed any conduct on his part, was altogether without good effect, the Governor announced that he had "obtained leave from the King to go to England." . . . It was his expectation that after a brief absence, when General Gage by a show of military force should have brought the province to a reasonable frame of mind, he would return and assume again the responsibilities of his office. He never returned, but died in England on June 3, 1780, an unhappy and a homesick exile from the country which he loved.[22]

[22] *Ibid.*, p. 199.

VI

Mr. Everybody's Historian

Knowledge alone is not enough: the question of ends, of what to do with knowledge remains. . . . Science, and especially social science, will therefore perform its function in vain without the aid of a political ethics capable of discriminating the social values which knowledge should serve.[1]

❦ *The Eve of the Revolution* is filled with the tragic sense of life without being pessimistic; it is humane and sympathetic without being sentimental. What Becker said, essentially, was that men on both sides acted as they had to act. Though they were all good men according to their lights, their underlying emotions and desires brought them into conflict with one another. This is the kind of history Becker wanted to write. He hoped before he died "to write a story of the French Revolution which will convey to those who can read between the lines, the same idea on a larger scale." [2]

What good did he think this idea would do Mr. Every-

[1] Becker, "The Function of the Social Sciences," *Science and Man,* p. 269.
[2] Becker to Dodd, June 17, 1920.

man? Of course one might answer that he was not thinking about Mr. Everyman's needs at all. Dodd implied once that Becker did not share his feeling that "a knowledge of history spread over the total population" would improve society, but Becker's presidential address and his explanation of it to Dodd stress the historian's responsibility to write history that has meaning and interest for Mr. Everyman. Unlike Osgood (and, in fact, most professional historians), who begrudged time spent on improving the form of what they had to say, Becker thought it of the first importance to write well enough to be read—more important, even, than discovering new facts. If the historian's first duty is to have something meaningful to say, his second is to say it clearly enough to be heard. "Voltaire's great influence was due," Becker pointed out, "chiefly to the fact that everybody read his works eagerly because they were so well written." [3] Becker was not a crusader like Voltaire, and he hardly expected many to heed what he said, but he saw to it that his books were not neglected because they were unreadable. His books were read. Historians found in them a style to be envied and a view of history to be reckoned with. What did Mr. Everyman find?

Becker said in 1941 [4] that he had never written a popular book, and it is true that he never wrote a book that was to be found "on all the young ladies' dressing tables" as Macaulay is supposed to have done. Nevertheless, as scholarly books go, Becker's were popular: they paid for themselves and a little more besides. Anyway, if Mr. Everyman did not read *The Heavenly City*, his son was

[3] Becker, *Modern History*, pp. 192–193.
[4] *Declaration of Independence*, p. xvii.

altogether likely to be reading Becker's high school text-book.[5] What is more, he was even likely to be enjoying it. There is some evidence (in letters from high school teachers and students) that the young people for whom the book was intended were as pleased with it as the grownups. Sidney B. Fay, who read the unidentified manuscript for the publishers, described it as follows:

I think it is a marvelously interesting, lucid, and fascinat-[ing]ly simple story of complicated events, and I congratulate you on getting it. It seems to me a most happy combination of Will Rogers, Alice in Wonderland, and the most serious and solemn books on history (like my own for instance). One is intrigued by the paragraph headings alone to read on and on. . . . I should think the book would sweep the field, and if I were a prophet I should say the author ought to reap $50,000 in a few years. Anyway, I hope so, especially if it is Professor Becker, who is the only person I know capable of writing such a book.[6]

This textbook is the only book Becker wrote whose readers numbered in the ten thousands, but all his other books were read by people who do much to create public opinion—newspapermen, radio commentators, teachers, and politicians. After all, Mr. Everyman himself is not a great reader; he seldom finds time for anything beyond *Life* and the *Reader's Digest*, but he is influenced by a great many ideas "in the air."

Becker undoubtedly helped to launch some of the ideas about our past that are still in the air. What sort of inter-

[5] *Modern History* (1st ed.; New York: Silver Burdett, 1931). This book went through seven editions during Becker's lifetime.

[6] Fay to Robert D. Williamson, Silver Burdett Co., June 24, 1929. Copy sent to Becker.

pretation of events did he give? How did he explain the
coming of the American Revolution for instance? His approach in *The Eve of the Revolution* was not at all new.
He told a story full of people doing and saying things,
but of "social forces" and "economic determination of history" we see nothing. The economic interpretation of history was very much in fashion at the time he wrote; many
historians saw this approach as the prime need of the day.
"What a mistake to seek in material interests the sole explanation of men's acts," Becker murmured to himself.[7]
But he did not try to fight the trend of the times: "The
attempt to pack the human spirit in some or other odd
shaped syllogistic hand-bag never does any harm because
it is never successful. The bag bursts, or the fashions
change, and the human spirit goes on its way, as resilient
as ever." [8] But his own interpretation was not quite the
old, simple narrative that it might appear on the surface.
He was consciously trying to bring one of the newer
sciences of mankind—psychology—to the service of history, "but not many historians seem to notice it," he wrote
wistfully, "for the reason, I suppose, that I make no use
of technical jargon." [9]

His interpretation is psychological and biographical.
Of course we see that trade and taxes are important things
that the colonists and the ministers got upset about, but
we do not see the war coming as an inevitable conflict
between the metropolis and the province. Instead we see
Franklin and Grenville and Townshend (too clever by

[7] Notes, drawer 5.

[8] Becker, "Idealistic Forces in American History," *Dial*, LVI
(Feb. 16, 1914), 141.

[9] Becker to Merle Curti, Oct. 12, 1935.

half!) and Hutchinson and that "brace of Adamses," all with complex human motives. Economic motives count—John Adams is particularly annoyed with the Mother Country for closing the courts just as he was getting under way at the bar—but much more important were the idealized visions men had of themselves: Thomas Hutchinson's pride in his role as Royal Governor and Loyal Servant of the Crown; Samuel Adams' picture of himself as a new Brutus, as a man with a call to look after the public business, to frustrate tyrannical plots before they were hatched. Becker makes us look at these men in the light of his own understanding:

> In the late 18th c[entury] the literature of the age inspired largely from France made a kind of conventional ideal of "Liberty," "Liberty of Mankind," "Virtue," "Welfare of the Human Race," "Friend of Mankind," etc. and in [the] colonies many men put their ideas on as a man puts on the conventional thing in hats, not insincerely as a mask to his interest, but in a perfectly natural way. Men wish to be thought to possess as many noble sentiments & generous emotions as the next man. There was much of this unconscious idealizing of their own motives and sentiments by men like Adams, R H Lee and many others [Notes, drawer 5].

The habit of doing and thinking what is expected of you by others and what is worthy of your own ideals is a compelling force with human beings, Becker thought—perhaps the mainspring of most right and generous action. Even the wildest illusions men cherish about themselves often have the virtue of pulling their behavior up closer and closer to some ideal. Becker's whole contribution to his students, he imagined, was in believing that they could do more than they thought they could, which often resulted in their going ahead and doing even more than he thought they could. "Without our best illusions life would be a poor thing," he admitted, and so he allowed all men their illusions without calling them hypocrites.

Whatever place or period Becker wrote about, he always counted men more than their environment. He doubted the usefulness of blaming everything on "environment" and was tickled with Professor Charles H. Hull's response to a remark of that tenor. Hull blandly inquired, "But what do you mean by his environment? Do you mean his undershirt or the starry firmament?" [10] To Becker the important thing about man is his ability to escape his environment through his intelligence and imagination. His interest in ideas above events demanded emphasis on individuals in history. Although he sought to understand the characteristic thought of whole periods of history, he could reach it only through studying the few articulate men, especially men who, by "intending their minds" [11] in a certain direction, by giving strong expression to certain ideas, helped to determine the dominant thought of an age.

In this predilection Becker differed again from the New Historians who, aiming to write about the masses instead of the classes, dealt knowledgeably with census tables, maps, cost-of-living indexes, and all the multiform statistical information that modern welfare states spill out. One looks long and hard to find an honest-to-goodness

[10] Becker, "Learning and the Life of Man," *Return to Freedom*, pp. 6–7. Becker's memory was probably wrong—both George Sabine and Louis Gottschalk remember this remark as being made originally by Professor Burr.

[11] Becker liked this expression of John Locke's; cited in his lecture notes, box 3, and *passim*.

statistic in one of Becker's books, and, worse yet, when he wrote *The Beginnings of the American People,* he confessed in a letter to Dodd (January 7, 1915), "Personally, I don't care a hang whether there are any maps or not." However important geographical and economic factors were in history, and Becker did, from time to time, give them their due in a general way, he just could not work up any enthusiasm for writing about them. He was thrilled by Turner's passionate interest in the Old Cumberland Road, but somehow, for Becker, it could never become the "thread that would unravel the whole tangled skein of American history." Turner himself was a genuine inspiration to Becker, as he was to many of his students and colleagues, but Turner's particular interpretation of American history—his frontier thesis—was so far out of Becker's metier that it was unfruitful for him. He could repeat it, as he did in *The United States: An Experiment,* but he did not develop it. Becker's interest was in democracy, as Turner's was, but it did not lead him to study the American forest; it led him back to "Locke and Sidney, Bacon and Tillotsen, and the author of Cato's Letters"; [12] it led him indeed to books and ideas which *might* have been brought to the colonies on the "Susan Constant" and the "Mayflower."

Becker was concerned with the fate of democratic government in the twentieth-century United States; he was anxious about the possible future of a political system derived from eighteenth-century philosophy, a "humane and engaging faith" but a faith that "could not survive

[12] *Beginnings of the American People,* p. 197. *Cato's Letters* or *The British Cato* was a series of political papers by Thomas Gordon and John Trenchard published in London from 1720–1723.

the harsh realities of the modern world."[13] "What Is Still Living in the Philosophy of Thomas Jefferson?" is the title of one of Becker's last essays. It was the question he had been working at for a lifetime. He worried about the disappearance of the climate of opinion which had developed and sustained democratic virtues, as Turner worried about the disappearance of the frontier which he thought provided the social and economic basis for democracy. The generous contagion of the Progressive Movement infected Turner and his students in the days before the Great War and they felt their social responsibilities strongly. Becker described in 1912 the mood that prevailed during his apprenticeship:

During the last two decades there has been a revival of faith in the possibility of social regeneration, a revival, one might almost say, of the optimistic spirit of the eighteenth century. Out of the wreck of old creeds, there is arising a new faith, born of science and democracy, almost the only vital conviction left to us—the profound belief, namely, that society can, by taking thought, modify the conditions of life, and thereby indefinitely improve the happiness and welfare of all men. As this faith strengthens, it finds expression in the imperative command that knowledge shall serve purpose, and learning be applied to the solution of the "problem of human life."[14]

But Becker never was able to obey that command in the direct and confident way that he would like to have done. Even providing history that would "hold the lamp for conservative reform," which was all his teacher asked, was not the simple task it sounded. Becker's lamp tended to cast a rather diffuse light, not too useful for picking out a

[13] *Declaration of Independence*, pp. 278–279.
[14] American Sociological Society, *Publications*, VII, 95–96.

path. The trouble was he thought too much; he saw
dilemmas where less reflective, more single-hearted men
saw none. He was not quibbling in the favorite academic
way when he kept calling for a definition of Progress.
He saw that if we continued to think of democracy in
terms of liberty and individualism "the situation of the
disinherited grows worse every day." The weak, left to
shift for themselves, are at the mercy of the strong. Yet,
if we limit liberty to try to keep more of .equality, "only
the state can take such a task—we arrive at State Socialism." [15] Which way lies Progress? We don't know, said
Becker, but Progress is our religion.

There is a kind of horror that attaches in the popular mind to
the man who is not for Progress, advancement, etc. He is a
bad citizen and a bad man. He is guilty of incivism. Thus a
man who has not faith in the people, in democracy, but wishes
for the rule of the few, for the rule of the fit, is anathema. . . .
I myself, while having no great love for democracy in many
of its manifestations, can scarcely get the Nietzschean point
of view, so bred in the bone is the theory of the welfare of
each and all, as the established basis of all ideas, without appeal.[16]

In the brightest days of the reform movement, Becker
was not uncritically enthusiastic about Progress; and yet
later, in the darker times between the two world wars
when everyone saw how romantic and naïve the faith had
been, he resisted taking easy, sardonic flings at "Progress."
A colleague, Professor Harry Caplan, remembers his in-
sisting that after all men had made life better in a number
of ways, even though in the process some of our problems
had become much more terrible.

The dilemma about political progress that Becker saw

[15] Notes, box 2.   [16] Undated, ca. 1900? Notes, drawer 9.

became ever clearer and more perplexing. How much liberty can we keep without sacrificing equality to such an extent that liberty becomes a mockery for the many? How much liberty can we curtail without achieving the dreary equality of the prison or the grave? Becker's taste was Jeffersonian: freedom above all else was his personal choice. "For me the satisfaction of being a heretic without being a martyr is not easily overestimated," [17] he wrote, but he feared that to other men with less nonconformist tendencies, and to hungry men of any tendencies, intellectual freedom did not matter much. He perhaps underestimated the strength of the average American's devotion to his "right to gripe." Whether he makes any use of his freedom to have unconventional ideas or not, the workingman may value as much as the professor his own right to sound off against the powers that be. All the same, Becker was undoubtedly correct in thinking a certain minimum of economic well-being must be secured by most men if democracy is to survive.

In the economic sense, there is for the great mass of men and women neither liberty nor equality. Without a much greater degree of both than now exists, the personal and political liberties which have been so hardly won through a century of struggle lose half their importance, and democracy itself is scarcely more than a pious hope.[18]

This was how it seemed to Becker in 1920; later, during the "depression decade," he was even more sure that the

[17] Becker, "The Dilemma of Liberals in Our Time," MS. This is one of several versions of a speech given at Columbia University, August 2, 1932. Parts of it appeared in several essays published later.

[18] *The United States: An Experiment,* p. 307.

capitalist system must be made to work more equitably or it would perish and drag down with it the whole structure of democratic government. Although Becker may have seemed safe in his ivory tower from the ravages of depression, he was in close touch with several of the unemployed and with young Ph.D.'s who were struggling to feed themselves and their wives on fourteen-dollar-a-week jobs. He understood quite well how they could look at the Soviet experiment with admiration, although he never could—being always deeply convinced that "in the long run, no freedom can be worth much that does not include freedom to discuss the ends & means of social organization." [19]

Becker got the usual treatment of moderates in times of stress—he was attacked from both the right and the left. The most sensational attack occurred during the Washington textbook investigation. An act of Congress, approved June 14, 1935, concerning appropriations for the District of Columbia, contained a proviso "that hereafter no part of any appropriation for the public schools shall be available for the payment of the salary of any person teaching or advocating communism." [20] On November 20, 1935, a committee of the Federation of Citizens Associations of the District of Columbia submitted to the Board of Education a memorandum declaring that communism was being taught in the public schools, specifically through three textbooks. One of them was Becker's *Modern History*. Mr. George E. Sullivan, chairman

[19] Becker to Max Lerner, March 25, 1938.
[20] Cited in the "Report of a Special Committee on Textbook Review," to the Board of Education of the District of Columbia, Dec. 18, 1935, p. 1 (mimeographed).

Carl Becker

of the Federation committee, was enthusiastically championed by the Hearst press. The Washington *Herald* headlined his description of Becker as a "well-known communist writer" and continued to play up his further pronouncements during the next few weeks.

Becker's publishers, Silver Burdett Company, chose to fight back, and, by representing to Becker that the school authorities needed help, they successfully urged Becker to defend himself against the charges. The episode ended in a complete vindication of Becker and his book. It was the accuser who was exposed as grossly ignorant and unfair. In those days few enough people were being investigated in Washington that a committee was actually set to read the books in question. The committee reported the context of each quotation which had been used as evidence of communism, and, by an intelligent reading, showed that none of these passages advocated communism. Professor (later Justice) Felix Frankfurter wrote Becker:

An attack on you of all people isn't funny—every decency in me is outraged that you should have to spend time and energy and money to fend off the passion and prejudices of people who haven't even a glimmering of a notion of the devotion and disinterestedness of your patriotism, if American patriotism means devotion to the gracious and humane purposes to which the great legends and heroes of America have dedicated their country [December 14, 1935].

A great many people felt as Frankfurter did and they deluged the Washington school board with letters and telegrams saying so, once they were nudged into action by wires (at Silver Burdett's expense) apprising them of the situation. The satisfactory outcome went a long way to console Becker's friends. "After all," wrote Frankfurter (January 11, 1936), "we are learning that liberty isn't a gift but a conquest."

Precisely while these charges were being leveled at Becker from the ranks of patrioteers, sharp judgments in the opposite vein came from the left. Louis Hacker considered the puzzling "case" of Becker in a review of *Everyman* in the *New Republic:*

Becker . . . embodies all the honest hesitancies and doubts of that vast group of American literate and trained white-collar workers who have at one and the same time always insisted upon their intellectual and professional independence and identified themselves economically with the middle class. . . . The extinction of all those things he holds dear must come if he and the middle-class intellectuals and professionals like him do not align themselves with the living forces in society.[21]

The *New Masses* thought still more poorly of Becker in 1941: "He is a liberal . . . with all the carefully guarded prejudices of the academic world. . . . He is like a man who goes to the edge of a precipice and looks over, then shuts his eyes and pretends that what he saw is not true." [22]

During the 1930's even Becker's most admiring students were distressed by his inactive role in politics.[23] Although he was convinced of the need for reform, Becker was very much the detached observer during the years be-

[21] Louis Hacker, "Historian of Revolutions," *New Republic,* LXXXV (Jan. 8, 1936), 260–261.

[22] Bruce Minton, review of *Modern Democracy, New Masses,* May 6, 1941.

[23] Val Lorwin to David Hawke, April 10, 1950. He was "disappointed that Becker wasn't a reformer."

tween the wars; he had always felt his part to be that of critic of proposed solutions rather than promoter. Both World Wars caused him to take up unaccustomed duties. In 1917–1918 he wrote several pamphlets on the historical background of the war for the National Board for Historical Service.[24] His disillusionment about the war perhaps made him more than ever dubious about direct social service. He thought "social scientists" were being very much misled by the name they had adopted for themselves if they thought they were experts in the art of living. Matter-of-fact knowledge had not entered the realm of human relations as yet, he pointed out. The subject matter of the social sciences—men—won't remain proper objects. They change their habits as a result of social theories that they learn, and this invalidates the theories.[25] The rumored plight of certain anthropologists who lately went out from Cornell to observe Navajo customs, is a case in point. The experts found the Indians, who have become favorite objects of study, conversant with all the latest anthropological theories and jargon and quite ready to give the desired answers to questions as soon as they discovered what university (and thereby what school of thought) the questioner came from. How fortunate indeed is the physicist that "the atom cannot acquire a knowledge of physics" [26] and physicists!

[24] Becker, "German Attempts to Divide Belgium," *A League of Nations*, I (Aug., 1918), 307–342; Becker, *America's War Aims and Peace Program* ("War Information Series," no. 21; [Washington?]: Committee on Public Information [1918]).

[25] Becker to Gottschalk, Sept. 3, 1944. Cf. Becker to the editor of the *New Republic*, LXXXV (Jan. 8, 1936), 256.

[26] Becker, *New Liberties for Old*, p. 15.

Mr. Everybody's Historian

One of Becker's most penetrating reviewers said that Becker diagnosed acutely the trouble with liberal historians, but that he had no cure to offer. Seeing that history must serve a purpose, he did not know "what purpose to put it to unless it be to show that for us it can have no purpose." Becker demonstrated, he thought, that "even though we realize that to be effective we must believe in something, there is not much in which we can believe, for we know, deny it verbally as we will, that the things we could believe in have already been tried and found wanting." In short, he said, Becker cannot find in history any significance for the liberal.[27] This judgment was not unjust at the time it was written—1935. As much as he disliked the idea, Becker very much feared that liberalism was only "a way station . . . on the main traveled road of human history." [28] The predicament of the liberal was so sharp that he could see no hope of escape. "Having been long enamored of both liberty and equality, we are now ever more insistently urged . . . to choose between them." Liberty had allowed oppressions to emerge that the liberal could not choose but denounce; equality legislated in Bolshevik style robbed the liberal of his most prized possession. Becker was convinced in the 1930's and remained convinced that "the economic liberty of the individual is intimately associated with his liberty of speech and the press." [29] He believed, as the political philosopher T. V. Smith phrased it in 1949, that "private

[27] Eliseo Vivas, review of *Everyman His Own Historian, Nation*, CXL (April 24, 1935), 487–488.

[28] "Liberalism—A Way Station," *Everyman*, p. 91.

[29] "Freedom of Speech," *Everyman*, p. 106; *Freedom and Responsibility*, p. 111.

property . . . was a bulwark for privacy of soul." [30] The choice between liberty and equality was dreadful. Worse still, Becker was convinced, it was illusory. Without liberty, equality would disappear just as surely as it would with unrestrained liberty.[31] Much of Becker's writing in the depression years has something of the aura of Thomas Hardy's *The Dynasts*.[32] Here is a sensitive man trying to prepare himself and us for a future that in the nature of things will be black. The Great Unrecking was quite possibly about to bring an end to the brief reign of liberal democracy. If so, let us at least enjoy our one superiority; man "alone can stand apart imaginatively and, regarding himself and the universe in their eternal aspects, pronounce a judgment." [33]

But most of the writing of Becker's lifetime was not on this cosmic level. When he was writing history, not writing about the writing of history, he found significance in man's past. Becker's one best seller—his *Modern History*—is his most stripped-down version of the story of mankind. Here we find the best proof that he never did doubt "that the defects of our democratic way of life, in comparison with the new order, are negligible, and that its liberties are of all our possessions the ones we cherish most and least wish to surrender." [34] In *Modern History* Becker told a story of the development of modern civiliza-

[30] T. V. Smith, "Property of Privacy," *Virginia Quarterly Review*, XXV (Summer, 1949), 344.

[31] *Everyman*, p. 100.

[32] Not accidentally, perhaps. Geoffrey Bruun remembers that Becker seemed to find "some particular significance in *The Dynasts*" (letter from Geoffrey Bruun, Oct. 19, 1950).

[33] Becker, *Progress and Power*, p. 115.

[34] *New Liberties for Old*, p. xvi.

tion conceived as H. G. Wells conceived it, as "the common adventure of mankind." It was a story full of cruelty and ignorance, but it is full, too, of bright deeds, high thoughts, and amazing achievements. It was, on the whole, a story of progress, although the enormous danger arising out of our scientific and material progress is vividly shown—particularly in Chapter XVI on the machine. Becker's history shows, as Voltaire's did, "that the greatest advancement in knowledge and civilization occurred when there was greatest freedom of thought," [35] although Becker proceeded in a different spirit. His most appealing characters—Galileo, Newton, Voltaire, and Cavour —are people to whom freedom of thought is precious, people who not only feel humanely, but think well. He has no villains: he simply shows us that "good and evil are strangely blended in the human heart," and those who mean well often cause the greatest suffering.

Becker's *Modern History* is moderate and tolerant, yet definitely liberal and humanistic. By virtue of its moderation the book was adopted for use in public high schools in a great many cities. On the other hand, Becker's liberal, secular approach to history was obvious enough to rouse objections among Roman Catholics on some school boards. His treatment of indulgences in the first edition of *Modern History* offended Catholic members of the New York City board, and the book was approved only on condition that the section be reworded.[36]

Undoubtedly Becker thought a knowledge of history

[35] *Modern History*, p. 191.
[36] Robert D. Williamson (for Silver Burdett Co.) to Becker, July 21, 1931. Cf. Becker, *Modern History*, 1st ed., pp. 40–41, and later editions.

Carl Becker

would benefit society, and he meant to help spread such knowledge, but his hopes were very different from William E. Dodd's, all the same—not only in degree but in quality. Dodd believed all his life—with ever greater urgency and passion—that "our people would know what to do to save our democracy" if only they could be given more knowledge and understanding of our past.[37] Becker was not so sure, but he thought that history had a profound value for the individual anyway:

The value of history is, indeed, not scientific but moral: by liberalizing the mind, by deepening the sympathies, by fortifying the will, it enables us to control, not society, but ourselves . . . it prepares us to live more humanely in the present and to meet . . . the future.

Dodd, an active citizen who always took vigorous part in party politics, thought of history as a branch of knowledge that would help men to decide and to act wisely; Becker, an observer who sometimes claimed he disliked even the responsibility of voting, valued history because it could help men to understand the world, though they could do little about it. At most, he thought that if men understood that they could not do much, nor do the little they could do fast, then they might save themselves from their greatest follies.

"One of the first duties of man is not to be duped, to be aware of his world," said Becker. One of the common-

[37] Dodd to Becker, Feb. 14, 1939. This was Dodd's last letter to Becker. It was written from the Georgetown Memorial Hospital a few months before the outbreak of the war that he knew was coming. It is a brief and moving testament of a man who sees that we have failed again to avert disaster, but who still believes we need not always fail.

Mr. Everybody's Historian

est and most dangerous ways in which men are duped is by believing that men deliberately cause and control events. If Mr. Everyman thinks bad things happen because bad men with bad motives conspire to make them happen, then he seeks simple remedies, and simple remedies in politics are apt to be violent ones, which create more problems than they solve. What Mr. Everyman needs is to understand *why* men have done the things they have done. To do this the historian needs above all else "a more subtle psychology," Becker thought.[38] He must show Mr. Everyman *why* revolutions come— not simply that autocratic rulers have been wicked, and brave men have overthrown them; or that good and wise statesmen have been defeated by clever conspirators. Mr. Everyman should be shown that even with the best possible luck our best hopes have been betrayed, not by men, but by history; "history is a cynical, tough old nut that always betrays our ideal aspirations." [39] Knowing these things, Mr. Everyman could better accept the compromises that life, particularly democratic life, demands of all men. Seeing through the eye of imagination other men, even the greatest of them, struggling to shape events and finally being shaped by them, Mr. Everyman can learn "to live more humanely" in the present. Most of all, he may find that if history shows anything it shows that progress is to be found in the "separation of the inner from the outer man, and in the subordination of material to spiritual values." [40] It may not give him the answer to the riddle of life, but "learning is essential to

38 Becker to Dodd, undated (ca. 1922?).
39 Becker to Gottschalk, Dec. 26, 1938 (Gottschalk files).
40 *Unpopular Review,* VII, 12.

the life of man because it is only through learning that the environment which conditions the thought and conduct of men can be . . . expanded and enriched." [41]

In the last years of his life it was this aspect of history that most interested Becker—history, "regarded as the sense of the past," enriching and expanding man's life.

Man is the only creature that has memory . . . that knows death, that sees himself as one of an interminable line of creatures who are born, struggle, & die to be succeeded by others who in their turn struggle & die. He asks why? What then is he to do with his memory? Use it merely for the purpose of living? Merely to recall what he did yesterday, & what he is to do today. . . . No. Life on those terms, since he knows death, is intolerable. He must enlarge this specious present and make it glorious. [42]

This is the high task of the historian, a task he shares with the theologian, the poet, the novelist, and the painter. "Holding the lamp" for some reform is no doubt a good thing—if it *does* turn out to be a reform, but this is an incidental benefit history may confer. It's real function is to give men a vision of themselves and their world, a vision that differentiates men from the animals.

"Now that I am old," wrote Becker in 1938, "the most intriguing aspect of history turns out to be neither the study of history [i.e., research] nor history itself [the meaning of events] . . . but rather the study of the history of historical study." [43] He outlined this thought in the essay "What Is Historiography?," which was occasioned by his reviewing Harry Elmer Barnes's book *The History of Historical Writing*. The book was concerned

[41] "Learning and the Life of Man," *Return to Freedom*, p. 7.
[42] Notes, drawer 2.   [43] *AHR*, XLIV (Oct., 1938), 20.

chiefly with estimating the "contributions of the major historical writers." That is what historiography is, says Becker, but it could be something quite different, and, though not so useful to the Ph.D. candidate, something very interesting and worth while. It could be the study of "what men at different times have known and believed about the past"; the study of "the growth and expansion of the time and space frame of reference" [44] from the narrow cramped world stone-age man carried in his mind, to "the universe of infinite spaces," [45] which is the achievement of modern man.

The historiographer who took this approach would "begin with the oldest epic stories—the Babylonian *Creation Epic*, Homer's *Iliad*, and the like." [46] He would give no more importance to true stories than false ones. The sweep of imagination is what he would be interested in —whether it led to fantasy or the mastery of matter-of-fact knowledge. How has man made his life glorious in past times? The springs of illusion and aspiration have nourished every product of man's intelligence. These are the sources of human power that Becker sought in individuals and nations and epochs.

In *The Heavenly City of the Eighteenth Century Philosophers*, published in 1932, he had presented for that period the kind of historiography he commended to our attention in 1938. A drawer of his latest notes indicates that he had laid down the factual foundation in his mind for a complete history of history, beginning with the *Iliad*. He taught a historiography course during his last few years before retirement which was evidently based on

[44] *Ibid.*, pp. 22, 25.   [45] *Progress and Power*, p. 116.
[46] *AHR*, XLIV, 27.

these notes and the outlines which accompany them. If he had lived a few more years, or if the crisis of the war had not called him into writing lectures and essays on current pressing questions, the essence of all this reading and pondering might have appeared in a slender book as timeless as *Progress and Power*, as far from orthodox history as *The Heavenly City*, of which Becker said: "This certainly isn't history. I hope it's philosophy, because if it's not it's probably moonshine:—or would you say the distinction is over subtle?" [47] Moonshine or philosophy, history or myth—what does it matter if it helps men to find "enduring values" amid "perishing occasions?" [48]

[47] Becker, autograph on flyleaf of *The Heavenly City*, presented to T. V. Smith, Oct. 11, 1932.
[48] Becker, review of *Adventures of Ideas*, by Alfred North Whitehead, *AHR*, XXXIX (Oct., 1933), 89.

Bibliography

WORKS BY CARL BECKER

Books

America's War Aims and Peace Plans. "War Information Series, no. 21"; [Washington?]: Committee on Public Information, 1918.

The Beginnings of the American People. "The Riverside History of the United States," vol. I. Ed. by William E. Dodd. 4 vols. Boston: Houghton Mifflin, 1915.

Cornell University: Founders and the Founding. Ithaca, N. Y.: Cornell University Press, 1943.

The Declaration of Independence: A Study in the History of Political Ideas. 2d ed. New York: Knopf, 1942.

The Eve of the Revolution. "Chronicles of America." New Haven: Yale University Press, 1918.

Everyman His Own Historian: Essays on History and Politics. New York: Appleton-Century-Crofts, 1935.

Freedom and Responsibility in the American Way of Life. New York: Knopf, 1945.

The Heavenly City of the Eighteenth-Century Philosophers. New Haven: Yale University Press, 1932.

The History of Political Parties in the Province of New York, 1760–1776. University of Wisconsin Bulletins, History Series, vol. II, no. 1. Madison, Wis.: University of Wisconsin, 1909.

Modern History. New York: Silver Burdett, 1931.

Bibliography

New Liberties for Old. New Haven: Yale University Press, 1941.

Progress and Power. 2d ed. New York: Knopf, 1949.

The United States: An Experiment in Democracy. New York: Harpers, 1920.

Articles and Reviews

"Benjamin Franklin," *Dictionary of American Biography.* Vol. VI.

"Detachment and the Writing of History," *Atlantic Monthly,* CVI (1910), 524–536.

"The Function of the Social Sciences," *Science and Man.* Ed. Ruth Nanda Anshen. New York: Harcourt, Brace, 1942.

"German Attempts to Divide Belgium," *A League of Nations,* I (1918), 307–342.

"Idealistic Forces in American History [Review of *The Power of Ideals in American History,* by Ephraim Douglas Adams]," *Dial,* LVI (1914), 140–142.

"An Interview with the Muse of History [Review of *Clio, a Muse,* by G. M. Trevelyan]," *Dial,* LVI (1914), 336–338.

"Learning and Teaching," *Cornell Contemporary,* II (1930), 13–14.

"Learning and the Life of Man," *Return to Freedom.* Ed. Thomas H. Johnson. New York: Putnam's, 1944.

Letter to the Editor, *Dial,* XLIX (1910), 454.

Letter to the Editor, *New Republic,* LXXXV (1936), 256.

Letter to the Editor [in answer to query about what books had most influenced his thinking], *New Republic,* XCVII (1938), 135.

"The New History [Review of *The New History,* by James Harvey Robinson]," *Dial,* LIII (1912), 19–22.

"A New Philosophy of History [Review of *The Interpretation of History,* by L. Cecil Jane]," *Dial,* LIX (1915), 146–148.

Bibliography

"On Being a Professor," *Unpopular Review*, VII (1917), 342–361.

"Progress," *Encyclopedia of the Social Sciences.* Vol. XII, 1934.

"The Reviewing of Historical Books," American Historical Association, *Annual Report*, 1912. Washington, 1914. Pp. 127–136.

"Some Aspects of the Influence of Social Problems and Ideas upon the Study and Writing of History,".American Sociological Society, *Publications*, VII (1913), 73–101.

"The Spirit of '76," *The Spirit of '76 and Other Essays*, by Carl Becker, J. M. Clark, and William E. Dodd. Washington: Robert Brookings Graduate School of Economics and Government, 1927.

"What Is Historiography?" *American Historical Review*, XLIV (1938), 20–28.

"What Is Still Living in the Political Philosophy of Thomas Jefferson?" American Philosophical Society, *Proceedings*, LXXXVII (1943), 201–210.

Review of *Adventures in Ideas*, by Alfred North Whitehead, *American Historical Review*, XXXIX (1933), 87–89.

Review of *The Idea of Progress*, by J. B. Bury, *American Historical Review*, XXXVIII (1933), 304–306.

Review of *The Problem of Historical Knowledge*, by Maurice Mandelbaum, *Philosophical Review*, XLIX (1940), 361–364.

Unpublished Material

Becker Papers. This collection in the Cornell University Library consists of correspondence (mostly letters received), manuscripts, and notes. It is contained in a large four-drawer steel letter file, a twenty-drawer filing cabinet for 4 x 6 notes, and six cardboard boxes of notes. Besides the papers left to the University by Becker, many of Becker's

Bibliography

correspondents have contributed letters they received from Becker to the collection. The manuscripts of many of Becker's books and articles are in the files, as well as a few unpublished manuscripts. There is also a small cardboard letter case containing clippings of Becker's reviews. This includes many reviews that were published unsigned to which Becker has added his signature.

SECONDARY SOURCES

Books

Asubel, Herman. *Historians and Their Craft.* New York: Columbia University Press, 1950.

Barnes, Harry Elmer. *History of Historical Writing.* Norman, Okla.: University of Oklahoma Press, 1937.

Curti, Merle, and Carstensen, Vernon. *The University of Wisconsin, 1848–1925.* 2 vols. Madison, Wis.: University of Wisconsin Press, 1949.

Fite, Warner. *Moral Philosophy.* New York: Dial Press, 1925.

Gottschalk, Louis. *Understanding History.* New York: Knopf, 1951.

James, Henry. *Art of Fiction and Other Essays.* New York: Oxford, 1948.

Jusserand, Jean Jules, and others. *The Writing of History.* New York: Scribner's, 1926.

Mandelbaum, Maurice. *The Problem of Historical Knowledge.* New York: Liveright, 1938.

Orwell, George. *Nineteen Eighty-Four.* New York: Harcourt, Brace, 1949.

Santayana, George. *The Life of Reason.* Vol. V. New York: Scribner's, 1906.

Vaihinger, Hans. *The Philosophy of 'As If.'* Tr. by C. K. Ogden. London: Keegan Paul, Trench, Trubner and Co., 1924.

Bibliography

Articles

Beard, Charles A. "That Noble Dream," *American Historical Review*, XLI (1935), 74–87.

——. "Written History as an Act of Faith," *American Historical Review*, XXXIX (1934), 219–231.

Destler, Chester McArthur. "Contemporary Historical Theory," *American Historical Review*, LV (1950), 503–529.

Dunning, William A. "Truth in History," *American Historical Review*, XIX (1914), 217–229.

Fling, Fred M. "Historical Synthesis," *American Historical Review*, IX (1903), 1–22.

Ford, Guy Stanton. "Carl Lotus Becker," *Yearbook of the American Philosophical Society*, 1945. Philadelphia, 1946. Pp. 338–346.

Gottschalk, Louis. "Carl Becker: Skeptic or Humanist?" *Journal of Modern History*, XVIII (1946), 160–162.

Smith, Theodore Clark. "The Writing of History in America, from 1884 to 1934," *American Historical Review*, XL (1935), 439–449.

Strout, Cushing. "Historical Thought in America," *Virginia Quarterly Review*, XXVIII (1952), 242–257.

Turner, Frederick Jackson. "Social Forces in American History," *American Historical Review*, XVI (1911), 217–233.

Van Tyne, Claude H. Review of *The Eve of the Revolution*, by Carl Becker, *American Historical Review*, XXIV (1919), 734–735.

Vivas, Eliseo. Review of *Everyman His Own Historian*, by Carl Becker, *Nation*, CXL (1935), 487–488.

[Willis, E. R. B.] "Carl Lotus Becker," in Cornell University, *Necrology of the Faculty, 1944–1945*. Ithaca, N.Y., 1945.

Bibliography

Reports

Report of a Special Committee on Text-book Review to the Board of Education of the District of Columbia, December 18, 1935. [Washington, 1935.]

Unpublished Material

Hawke, David. "Carl Becker." Unpublished Master's thesis, Department of History, University of Wisconsin, 1950.

Horwich, Carl. "Carl Becker—A Study of Liberalism and the History of Ideas." Unpublished Master's thesis, Department of History, Wayne University, 1941.

Index

Absolutes, unreal, 35
Adams, Herbert Baxter, 48
Adams, James Truslow, 41n.
Adams, John, 162
Adams, Samuel, 162, 168, 171ff.
Adventures of Ideas (Whitehead), 212n.
American Historical Association, 83
American Sociological Society, 62, 68, 198n.
Anna Karenina (Tolstoy), 3, 137, 148
Aristotle, 144
Art, superiority of, 127
"Art of Writing, The" (Becker), 4n.
Asubel, Herman, 117n.
Aulard, François Victor Alphonse, 129

Bancroft, George, 163
Barnes, Harry Elmer, 70n., 77, 114, 118ff.
Beard, Charles A., 48n., 91, 111ff., 114-115, 118ff.
Becker, Carl:
  as controversial figure, 43
  as disciple of Hume, 35-37
  as literary artist, 132ff.
  as lover of fiction, 143
  as philosopher of history, 44

as poet, 14, 153ff.
as skeptic, 13-14, 32, 121
boyhood of, 3, 133
catholic taste of, 142ff.
college years of, 5-15
communism charged, 201-202
compared to Jefferson, 163ff.
death of, 32
disillusionment of, 152ff.
forebears of, 1
illnesses of, 28-29
in Kansas, 133
interest in history of, 6
ironic humor of, 84
journals of, 149ff.
loss of faith of, 13-14
MSS and correspondence of, 2n.
marriage of, 17
notes of, 149ff.
no logician, 107ff.
no orator, 28
no reformer, 203ff.
no scientific historian, 45
no showman, 26-27
"On Being a Professor," 10n.
on Beneficent Providence, 2, 14
on euphony, 167
on revolution, 169
on teaching, 23-27
personal qualities, 6, 35ff.

Index

Index

Index

222

Index

Index

Index

William W. Cook Foundation, 30
Willis, E. R. B., 2n., 134n.
Will to believe, 124
Wilson, Woodrow, 40, 168
Wisconsin, University of, 44, 48, 49, 56, 146
Woolf, Virginia, 144
Wordsworth, William, 164
World War I, 40, 168
World War II, 34
"Writer's malady," 135, 145
Writing:
  advice on, 138ff., 145ff., 157-158
  ambition for, 6, 132
  art of, 131ff., 133n., 135ff.

Becker's own story of, 136ff.
chosen as career at eleven, 16
definition of, 137-138
done by ear, 138-139
illustrated, 173ff., 176ff.
persistence in, 136ff.
practice of, 167ff.
rules for, 167ff.
technique of, 158ff.
turned to historical content, 45
"Written History as an Act of Faith" (Beard), 118-119

Zeno's paradoxes, 78n.